OECD Studies on Water

# Managing and Financing Water for Growth in Thailand

## HIGHLIGHTS OF A NATIONAL DIALOGUE ON WATER

**OECD**

BETTER POLICIES FOR BETTER LIVES

This document, as well as any data and map included herein, are without prejudice to the status of or sovereignty over any territory, to the delimitation of international frontiers and boundaries and to the name of any territory, city or area.

The statistical data for Israel are supplied by and under the responsibility of the relevant Israeli authorities. The use of such data by the OECD is without prejudice to the status of the Golan Heights, East Jerusalem and Israeli settlements in the West Bank under the terms of international law.

**Please cite this publication as:**
OECD (2022), *Managing and Financing Water for Growth in Thailand: Highlights of a National Dialogue on Water*, OECD Studies on Water, OECD Publishing, Paris, https://doi.org/10.1787/839a4f70-en.


ISBN 978-92-64-71799-2 (print)
ISBN 978-92-64-35387-9 (pdf)
ISBN 978-92-64-93114-5 (HTML)
ISBN 978-92-64-56814-3 (epub)


OECD Studies on Water
ISSN 2224-5073 (print)
ISSN 2224-5081 (online)

Photo credits: Cover © ONWR.

# Foreword

This report distils the main outcomes of the policy dialogue on water in Thailand, convened by the Asia Water Council, K-water and the OECD in 2021-22.

The Office of National Water Resources was the main counterpart in Thailand. ONWR coordinated data collection and stakeholder consultation. It provided expertise at every step of the process. The OECD and the Asia Water Council are grateful to ONWR for their constant support and engagement. In particular, Mr. Chumlarp Tejasen, Ms. Thayida S. van Corstanje and Dr. Wimolpat Bumbudsanpharoke Khamkanya, Foreign Affairs Division, played a critical role in moving the project forward.

The project was initiated in 2021. A fact-finding mission was arranged in December 2021. A policy seminar was convened by ONWR in March 2022, with delegates from several departments, regional authorities, industry and civil society. Comments received at the policy seminar are reflected in the final report.

The report was essentially drafted by Delia Sanchez Trancon and Taehoon Kim, under the supervision of Xavier Leflaive, Water Team lead, all working at the OECD Environment Directorate. Dr. Yongdeok Cho, Mr. Jaewon Lee and Ms. Gahae Choi, from the Asia Water Council provided substantive material, in particular on smart technologies, and valuable comments.

The OECD Working Party on Biodiversity, Water and Ecosystems was invited to comment on a draft report.

The project is part of a regional initiative with Korea, the Asia Water Council and the OECD, to support the achievement of water-related SDGs in 8 Asian countries, through a combination of country-specific policy dialogues and regional consultations.

The OECD gratefully acknowledges the Korean Ministry of Environment for the financial support for the project.

# Table of contents

## Tables

## Figures

## Boxes

---

## Follow OECD Publications on:

https://twitter.com/OECD

https://www.facebook.com/theOECD

https://www.linkedin.com/company/organisation-eco-cooperation-development-organisation-cooperation-developpement-eco/

https://www.youtube.com/user/OECDiLibrary

https://www.oecd.org/newsletters/

# Acronyms and abbreviations

| | |
|---|---|
| ADB | Asian Development Bank |
| AFD | Agence Française de Développement, France |
| ANA | Agência Nacional de Águas e Saneamento Básico, Brazil |
| AWC | Asia Water Council |
| DAC | Development Assistance Committee, OECD |
| DFI | Development Finance Institute |
| ECA | Export Credit Agency |
| EEC | Eastern Economic Corridor, Thailand |
| EIB | European Investment Bank |
| ICT | Information and Communication Technology |
| LGUGC | Local Government Unit Guarantee Corporation, Philippines |
| MDB | Multilateral Development Bank |
| MoE | Ministry of Environment, Republic of Korea |
| MoNRE | Ministry of Natural Resources and Environment, Thailand |
| MRC | Mekong River basin Commission |
| MWA | Metropolitan Waterworks Authority, Thailand |
| NRW | Non-Revenue Water |
| NWC | National Water Command, Thailand |
| NWRC | National Water Resources Committee, Thailand |
| ONWR | Office of the National Water Resources, Thailand |
| OUGC | Organismes Uniques de Gestion Collective, France |
| PWA | Provincial Waterworks Authority, Thailand |
| PWRF | Philippine Water Revolving Fund |
| RBC | River Basin Committee, Thailand |
| RID | Royal Irrigation Department, Thailand |
| RMF | River Management Fund, Republic of Korea |
| SPV | Special Purpose Vehicle |

| SWM | Smart Water Management |
| USAID | United States Agency for International Development |
| WMA | Wastewater Management Authority |
| WSS | Water Supply and Sanitation |
| WSUD | Water Sensitive Urban Design |

# Executive summary

The Kingdom of Thailand has achieved remarkable economic development over the last 6 decades. It aspires to become a high-income economy by 2037, as outlined in its 20-year national strategy. In order to achieve these objectives, the government is developing new growth hubs, starting with the Eastern Economic Corridor (EEC).

Water security and disaster risk management are requisites for this ambition to materialise. Considering Thailand's contribution to a number of global value chains, success in these areas have a global significance.

However, several water challenges coexist such as competitive increase in water demand in agriculture, industry and service sector; deterioration of water quality due to increasing pollutants; deepening damage from floods and droughts due to climate change - Thailand is recognised as highly vulnerable to climate variability and change - and management of rivers and aquifers shared across regions.

In that context, the Thai government embarked in a policy dialogue on water, supported by the OECD, the Asia Water Council and the Korean Ministry of Environment. The dialogue focused on two sets of issues: managing water demand in the Eastern Economic Corridor and financing water supply and sanitation. The first one is essential to support rapid economic growth in the region. The second contributes to better livelihoods and increased water quality nation-wide. Success in both areas can build on recent developments, but also require significant adjustments in water policies and policies that affect water availability and demand.

Water supply in the EEC is ensured through a complex system of reservoirs and distribution lines across the region and neighbourhood provinces. The long-term forecast for the Eastern region indicates that the area is exposed and vulnerable to climate change. Rising sea levels can also introduce new, or exacerbate existing, saltwater intrusion into freshwater resources. Both groundwater and surface water sources are at risk. The dialogue highlighted that enhanced water security in the EEC would benefit from supplementing water supply augmentation (already locked in development plans) by a range of measures, combining robust water allocation regimes, stimulating demand for reclaimed water and fair compensation for provinces which water is diverted to augment supply in the EEC. The diffusion of a range of smart water technologies would seem appropriate in that context.

Allocation regimes in the EEC would benefit from robust data on water use and availability – the One Map programme goes in the right direction - on which to build licences to abstract water (including for agriculture) and related economic instruments; licences should also factor return flows in. In addition, a thorough definition – and enforcement - of environmental flows would contribute to water security and other benefits.

Access to water supply and sanitation has steadily improved in Thailand. However, in 2020, only 26% of the population was using safely managed sanitation services and only 24% of the wastewater flow was safely treated. This situation contributes to water pollution and to raising costs to use water. Additional investment is required to collect and treat wastewater and to address further cost drivers, including population growth and urbanisation, economic growth (and raising social expectations) and the need to adapt to a changing climate. It is not clear how these drivers are reflected in Thai plans to extend coverage and improve quality of service, in both urban and rural settings.

To cover such investment needs, number of requisites need to be in place. The first is operational efficiency of existing services, a condition to efficient allocation of (public and private) funding, willingness to pay of domestic water users, and minimising financing needs in the future (avoiding rapid decay of existing assets). Economic regulation has a role to play: systematic benchmarking of the performance of service providers can be the basis of tailored incentives towards operational efficiency. International experience can inspire the selection of performance indicators and the design of incentives, including through performance-based contracting. Smart water technologies can support such an endeavour.

When the enabling conditions are in place, blended finance can play a critical role in mobilising the commercial finance required as well as strengthening the financing systems upon which water–related investments rely. Commercial finance is all the more relevant when public finance is constrained. Thailand is no exception in this domain: in the aftermath of the pandemic, the debt-to-GDP ratios of most Emerging Asian countries are expected to continue rising in 2022; calls from across society for measures to address longer-term challenges such as climate change – which essentially translates into water issues - will also lead to continued demands on government spending. This puts further constraints on public finance. More work is required to assess whether the enabling conditions are in place. The prospects are promising as private investment in the water sector could benefit from Thailand's track record in investment attraction, and proactive investment promotion and facilitation policies under a strong Board of Investment.

Partners in the water dialogue acknowledge that some needed reforms are sensitive and challenging: water allocation regimes, standards and incentives for reclaimed water, the enabling conditions to attract commercial finance for water supply and sanitation investments. The OECD, the Asia Water Council and the Korean Ministry of Environment stand ready to further collaborate with ONWR and Thai authorities to move further ahead and make water a driver for sustainable growth in Thailand.

# 1 Background and objectives

The policy dialogue is a demand-driven process, focused on two pillars identified as priorities by ONWR and Thai partners. The two pillars are water demand management in the Eastern Economic Corridor, and financing water supply and sanitation.

The National Dialogue on Water in Thailand aims to support adjustments in water resources management, building on the agenda that Thailand has embarked upon in recent years (e.g. the new Water Resources Act, and the Master Plan on Water Resources Management). Representatives from ONWR (Office of the National Water Resource) and other Thai stakeholders have indicated that it is a priority to address the policy, institutional, financial and technical challenges related to enhancing water security and improving efficiency in Thailand, particularly in the rapidly developing Eastern Economic Corridor (EEC)[1].

The Dialogue's scope is confined to two main topics, which reflect initial discussions with the Government of Thailand (e.g. ONWR) and Thai stakeholders:

1. **Water demand** management – This includes a particular focus on improving water allocation regimes in the EEC and the design of economic instruments such as water tariffs and water charges to incentivise behaviour change. Further discussions with Thai authorities highlighted the following priorities:

   - Robust water allocation regime to minimise conflicts during scarcity time in the EEC, including cost-effective compensation measures to inter-basin water transfers
   - Reuse of treated wastewater for households, agriculture and industry in the EEC, in particular how to improve and incentivise the perception of potential water re-use users in all sectors.

2. Financing **water supply and sanitation** – This includes a focus on taxes and tariffs for water supply and sanitation services, in coordination with policies and incentives to enhance the performance of utilities and independent economic regulation in this domain. More specifically, Thai authorities requested recommendations on:

   - Benchmarking the performance of water utilities in the country
   - An additional variable in the new tariff for funding compensation measures for users who have been affected by planned water security measures
   - Best practices and examples of blended finance for water supply and sanitation services.

These topics are the focus of the analysis of water-related policy, financing and institutions )OECD-led(, in parallel with analysis of relevant water technologies and innovation )AWC-led(.

Thai authorities have shared with project partners a background report that characterises the state of play as regards the two topics listed above. They also provided detailed information in response to a questionnaire put together by the project partners. Building on this knowledge base, the project partners sketched a list of issues to be investigated further in the context of the Dialogue, in order to address the two main topics. This document builds on information compiled and previous conversations on these issues.

Notes

[1] The EEC is a special economic zone off the coast of the Gulf of Thailand, which encompasses the three provinces of Chonburi, Rayong and Chachoengsao and is facing significant water security and water demand challenges.

# 2 Water resources management in Thailand

Thailand has achieved remarkable economic and social development over the last 50 years. The sustainability of this strategy over the longer term requires – among other things - a robust capacity to adapt to climate change and in particular to mitigate water-related risks. Water scarcity is a case in point, as it can hinder the development of the fast growing Eastern Economic Corridor (EEC).

The chapter synthesises water-related issues in Thailand and the EEC. It characterises the prevailing response, essentially water supply augmentation.

## 2.1. Country profile

The Kingdom of Thailand has made remarkable economic development visible through energy, transport and tourism sectors. Strong growth since the 1970s enabled the country to join the group of upper-middle-income economies in the early 2010s. Thailand aims to become high-income economy by 2037 enjoying "Security, Prosperity and Sustainability" according to its 2017 National Strategy Preparation Act. Therefore, Thailand is striving for enhancing its economic competitiveness and social advancement to become one of the leading countries in South East Asia (OECD, 2019[1]).

Effective water resources management - including flood control, irrigation and water supply - is a condition for economic success and the ambitious vision can be jeopardised by Thailand's increasing water insecurity. Growing population, economic growth, rapid urbanization and the looming threats posed by climate change are expected to make sustainable water management significantly more difficult in the coming years. By 2030, Thailand's population is projected to reach about 71–77 million, with an increasing proportion living in urban areas (The World Bank Group and the Asian Development Bank, 2021[2]). In 2020, the urbanisation rate reached 51.43% of the total population, showing a change of life pattern leading to an increase in water demand (Ta and Watershed, 2008[3]). Thailand's economy is 90% based on the industrial and service sector, with the agricultural sector accounting for only 10%, but representing 33% of the workforce (The World Bank Group and the Asian Development Bank, 2021[2]). Water productivity is low in all sectors in Thailand, but in particular in agriculture (where it is almost nil); as comparison the industry sector reaches around 60 USD per $m^3$ (Chokchai , and Sucharit, 2019[4]). The Eastern area is the second area with the highest water productivity for all sector 12.73 USD per $m^3$, however being almost 5 time lower than Bangkok region (Chokchai , and Sucharit, 2019[4]). In addition, in the Eastern area, the industry sector has the highest water productivity rate of the country, namely 76.41 USD per $m^3$.

Thailand is recognised as highly vulnerable to climate variability and change due to increasing natural hazards, such as heavy rainfall, floods, and droughts. In addition, sea level rise affects the country's coasts. The country ranked in the 31th position in National Water Security Index among 49 Asian and Pacific countries mainly due to a low water urban security and high climatological risks (Asian Development Bank, 2020[5]). The Intergovernmental Panel on Climate Change reports that global sea level rise associated with climate change is expected to be between 8 - 16 mm/year in the 21st century. Due to global climate change, sea level in the inner part of the Gulf of Thailand is expected to increase in the future. The increase in wind speed, and especially of the monsoons that blow into the Gulf of Thailand, adds to the rising sea level. (The World Bank Group, 2021[6]).

Several water challenges coexist such as competitive increase in water demand in agriculture, industry and service sector, deterioration of water quality due to increasing pollutants, deepening damage from floods and droughts due to climate change, and management of rivers and aquifers shard across regions.

Floods are by far the greatest natural hazard facing Thailand in terms of economic and human impacts. Thailand is cited as one of the ten most flood-affected countries in the world. Drought and cyclone impacts also represent major hazards. All may intensify in future climate scenarios. The number of people affected by an extreme river flood could grow by over 2 million by 2035–2044, and coastal flooding could affect a further 2.4 million people by 2070–2100. Projections suggest that Thailand's agriculture sector could be significantly affected by a changing climate, due to its location in the tropics where agricultural productivity is particularly vulnerable to temperature rises (The World Bank Group and the Asian Development Bank, 2021[2]).

The long-term forecast for the Eastern region indicates that the area is exposed and vulnerable to climate change. Rising sea levels can also introduce new, or exacerbate existing, saltwater intrusion into freshwater resources. Both groundwater and surface water sources are at risk (Petpongpan, Ekkawatpanit and Kositgittiwong, 2020[7]).

Thailand is focusing its adaptation efforts in key sectors such as energy, water, transportation, agriculture, human settlements and public health, according to the submitted the Third National Communication to the United Nations Framework Convention on Climate Change in 2018, its Initial Nationally Determined Contribution in 2016 and its Updated Nationally Determined Contribution in 2020 (The World Bank Group and the Asian Development Bank, 2021[2]).

## 2.2. Institutional arrangements and strategies of Thailand's water resources management

The prevailing institutional organisation for water management in Thailand is complex and may lead to overlaps and inconsistencies, as presented in Table 2.1. . This is detrimental to effective policy making and cost-effective investments, as it can hinder policy coherence across jurisdictions (across policy areas and across levels of governments). Based on Thai authorities' priorities, this Dialogue will not review the arrangements in detail. This could be the focus of a subsequent project, should there be an interest.

According to the Water Resources Act 2018, the National Water Resources Commission is in charge of water resources regulation[1]. Since the creation of the ONWR, Thailand has 22 major rivers basins Committees and 353 small and medium river basins.

Water and sanitation services are provided by public utilities across the countries (Table 2.2.), with few exceptions such as Eastwater a private entity operating in the EEC region. Currently, no agency is in charge of regulating water and sanitation service providers.

Table 2.1. Major Water related Agencies

| No | Name | Scope | Supervisor | Missions |
|---|---|---|---|---|
| 1 | Office of National Water Resources (ONWR) | National | Prime Minister's office | proposing policies and formulating strategic plans, master plans and measures in national water resources management and coordinating for implementation |
| 2 | Ministry of Natural Resources and Environment (MONRE) | National | Prime Minister's office | preserve, conserve, develop, and rehabilitate natural resources and environment to ensure their sustainable use |
| 3 | Department of Water Resources (DWR) | National | Ministry of Natural Resources & Environment | formulating policy and plan as well as measures relating to water resources, management, development, conservation, rehabilitation |
| 4 | Pollution Control Department (PCD) | National | Ministry of Natural Resources & Environment | regulate, supervise, direct, coordinate, monitor and evaluate with respect rehabilitation, protection and conservation of environmental quality |
| 5 | Royal Irrigation Department (RID) | National | Ministry of Agriculture & Cooperative | development and conservation of water-related activities such as irrigation, drainage, land reclamation, flood control, water transportation on irrigation waterways |
| 6 | Department of Disaster Prevention and Mitigation (DDPM) | National | Ministry of Interior | draft National Disaster Prevention and Mitigation Plan |
| 7 | Electricity Generating Authority of Thailand (EGAT) | National | Ministry of Energy | generation and transmission of electricity including hydropower plant operation |
| 8 | River Basin Committee (RBC) | Regional | Headed by nominated governor | 1) Information/database; 2) Policy and planning; 3) regulation; 4) technical; 5) public relation and coordination; conflict resolution; and 7) monitoring and evaluation |

Source: Background Information Gathering and Fact Finding on Thailand Water-Related Challenges and Policy Agenda, ONWR, Thailand, 2021

## Table 2.2. Major Water Supply & Sanitation Agencies

| No | Name | Work Scope | Supervisor | Missions |
|----|------|-----------|-----------|----------|
| 1 | Metropolitan Waterworks Authority (MWA) | Regional (Bangkok) | Metropolitan Government of Bangkok | operating drinking water supply facilities for the citizens in the metropolitan area<br>expanding its service coverage into the area out of reach in Bangkok area |
| 2 | Provincial Waterworks Authority (PWA) | Regional (74 provinces) | Ministry of Interior | operating drinking water supply facilities for the citizens in the 74 provinces except Bangkok<br>expanding its service coverage into the area out of reach in 74 provinces |
| 3 | Local Government Authorities(LGAs) | Regional (small village) | Local Government | Constructing/ repairing the village water supply system<br>Restoring natural water sources which have a capacity of less than 2 million cubic meters<br>Improving water distribution system which has the capacity of less than 320 ha |
| 4 | Wastewater Management Authority (WMA) | Regional (74 provinces) | Ministry of Interior | Installing/ Constructing the community wastewater treatment system in the area that the local government has insufficient potential in entire country except Bangkok |
| 5 | Pollution Control Department (PCD) | National (including Bangkok) | Ministry of Natural Resources & Environment | Setting the guidelines and supporting the technical information, and setting benchmarking<br>Setting, monitoring and enforcing the law on sources of pollution |
| 6 | Department of Industrial Works | National (including Bangkok) | Ministry of Industry | Setting the water conservation measures for industrial factory<br>Monitoring and enforcing the laws on sources of pollution |
| 7 | Industrial Estate Authority of Thailand | National (including Bangkok) | Ministry of Industry | providing the public utility service which is necessary for the industry<br>Setting the water conservation measures for the industrial factory in the industrial estate |

Source: Questionnaire for the National Dialogue on Water in Thailand, ONWR, Thailand, 2021

Thai government has set water security as a top priority in the political agenda and has undertaken a major policy reform. The government reviewed the current framework through four main pillars, to set the direction in improving water management resources:

1. The 20 year Master Plan on Water Resources Management (2018 – 2037);
2. The creation of Office National Water Resources (ONWR);
3. Water Resources Act 2018; and
4. Developing a water management system.

## 2.3. Water development plan in the EEC

The Thailand 4.0 economic model aims to become high-income country. The four pillars of this strategy are economic prosperity, social well-being, raising human values and environmental protection. In order to achieve these objectives, the government is developing new growth hubs, starting with the Eastern Economic Corridor (EEC). The government is also set to accelerate the area's readiness to support all aspects of investment and economic growth, and expects that the EEC will be an important centre for trade, investment, regional transportation, and a strategic gateway to Asia. Thailand's government masterplan aims to develop the EEC region as the main hub of high-tech industries of the country. Developing new economic growth hubs including EEC needs stable and resilient social infrastructures to underpin well-functioning city mechanism such as sufficient and reliable energy, water and other public goods supply networks (EEC Office, 2019[8]).

The EEC covers three provinces (Chachoengsao, Chonburi and Rayong) with very different socio-economic and climatic conditions (Figure 2.1. ). In the north area of the EEC, Chachoengsau main economic sector is agriculture, producing mainly rice and aquaculture. According to ONWR, current water demand equals the supply, and water supply is ensured by numerous dams in the watershed. Rayong and Chonburi provinces contain the industrial and touristic development following the coastline, as well as the new cities. These two regions have limited water resources, and the current water demand is already higher than supply. Supply is ensured by small reservoirs in the area. Due to the climatic-topographic conditions, it is not possible to develop larger in-situ water storage.

Water supply in the EEC is ensured through a complex system of reservoirs and distribution lines across the region and neighbourhood provinces. Current and future sources of water in the EEC are reservoirs, as illustrated in Figure 2.2. .

Figure 2.1. EEC map

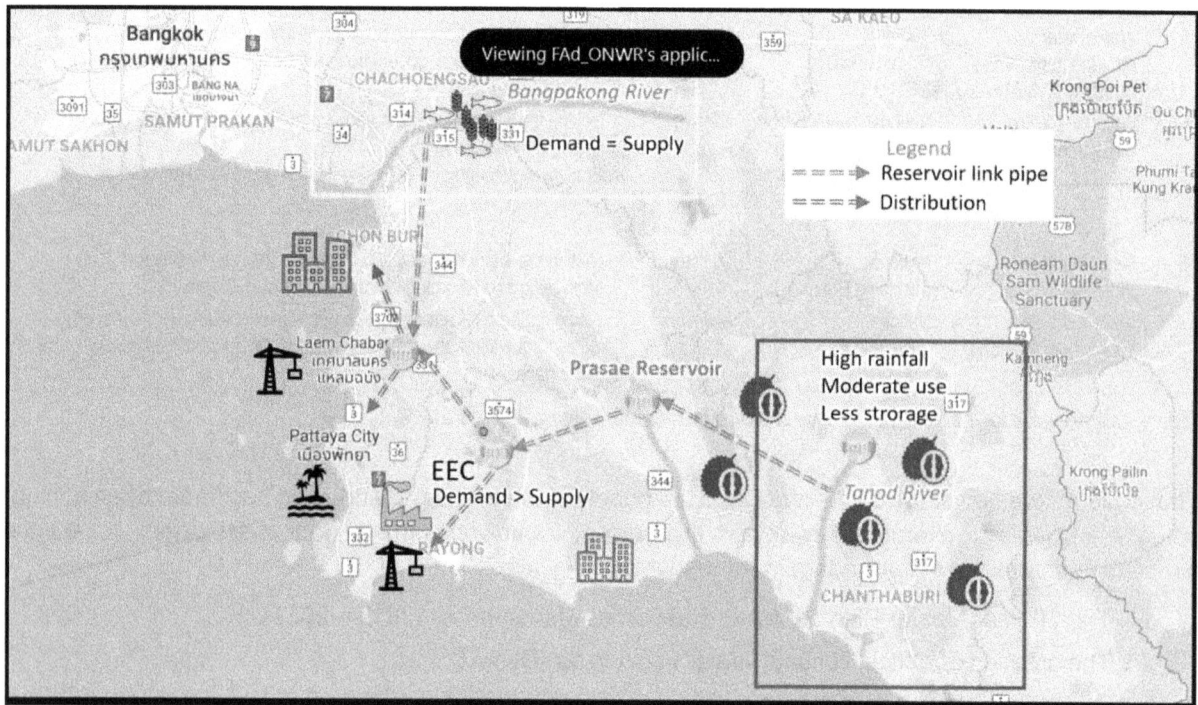

Source: Presentation during the ONWR interviews, 2022.

The Royal Irrigation Department is the main authority undertaking water allocation from reservoirs in the EEC, based on water availability in the reservoir and demands from all sectors. During normal runoff years, the current demands are met. However, during dry years, supply is insufficient to satisfy demand. Therefore, special measures have been put in place across sectors, such as reduction of rice land during the dry season and imposing water conservation measures. However, as forecast by Thai authorities demand will overpass supply in the future. During some periods of the year, this is already the case and restrictions need to be imposed on some users, mainly farmers.

The water development plan for the EEC was approved in 2020 (Figure 2.2.  and Box 2.1) which covers quality and quantity management elements aiming to ensure water security in the region.

## Figure 2.2. Water Resources Development Projects in EEC (2020-2037)

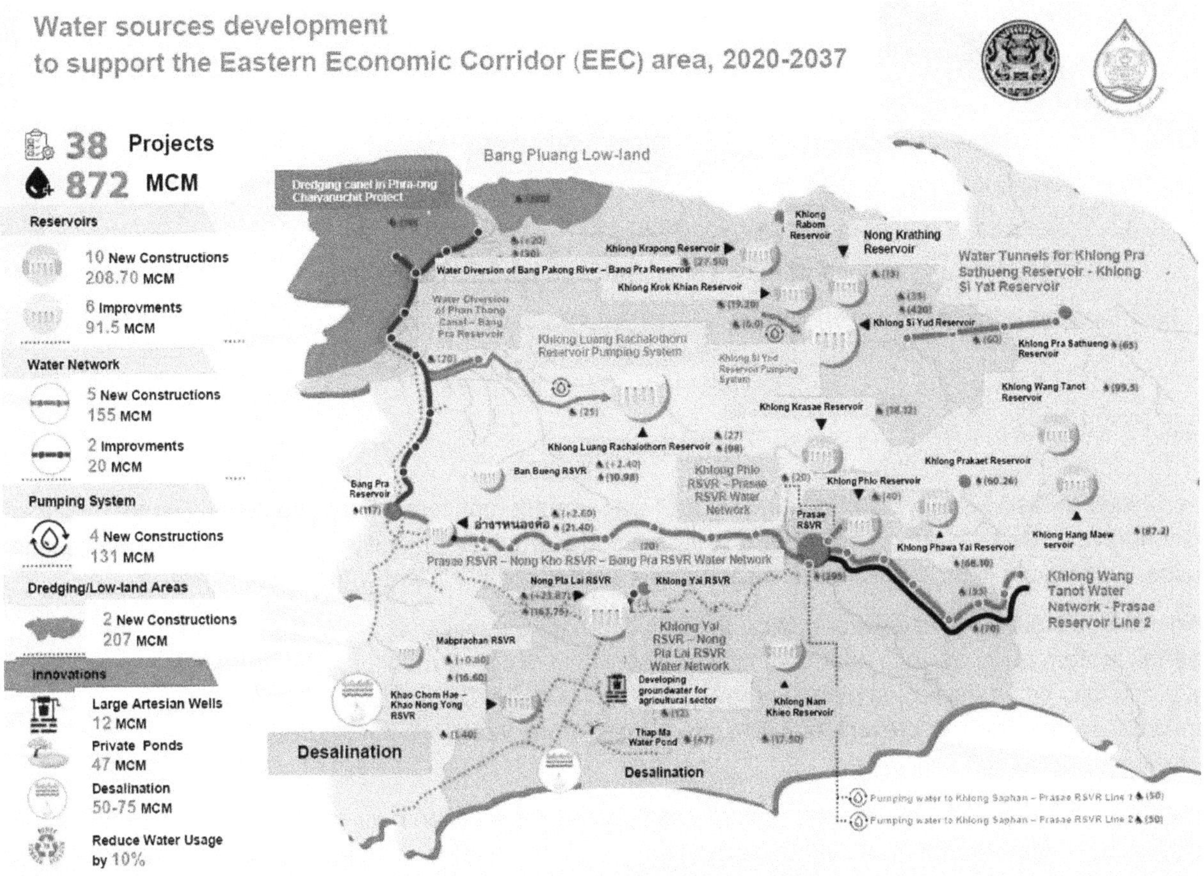

Source: Questionnaire for the National Dialogue on Water in Thailand, ONWR, Thailand, 2021

The EEC water management plan sets a short-term plan to prevent drought and a long-term plan to ensure *"environmentally friendly and sustainable water management"*. The short-term plan focuses mainly on increasing water supply through reservoirs and water diversions. Only one activity targets water demand management by aiming to reduce water usage from the industry sector by 10 percent (EEC Policy Committee, 2020[9]).

The long-term plan focuses on supply through reservoirs and diversions systems, reaching 50 thousand million Baht (1.5 thousand million USD). It considers as well desalination as potential additional source. The budget for demand management is almost 50 times lower (19 thousand million bath, 58 million USD) aiming to reduce losses through agriculture water usage plan, groundwater database and reinforcing the collaboration with the Provincial Waterworks Authority. In addition, it includes reservoir construction and water diversion system under the water management component (EEC Policy Committee, 2020[9]).

As illustrated in Figure 2.1. , according to Thai's government plan, Chanthaburi neighbouring province, with abundant water resources and agricultural sector producing high value crops, will be providing water to Prasae, the main reservoir in the EEC.

**Box 2.1. Water Resources Development and Management Project for the EEC**

1. Water resource development plan for 2020-2027, including 38 projects that will increase the amount of water availability by 872.19 mcm
2. Water demand management Plan for 2020-2037, 9 projects
3. Prevention and mitigation plan for 2020-2037, 25 projects,
4. Water quality management plan for 2020-2037, 33 projects
5. Other measures to cope with the water shortage between 2020-2037 for 3 projects

Source: Background Information Gathering and Fact Finding on Thailand Water-Related Challenges and Policy Agenda, ONWR, Thailand, 2021

## 2.4. Wastewater management in the EEC

In relation to water quality, the Pollution Control Department monitors inland and coastal water quality of Chonburi and Rayong provinces. Water quality is poor due to water pollution from domestic and industrial uses. Some point sources discharge wastewater, which is not compliant with the standard.

To manage industrial wastewater quality, the reduction of wastewater at point sources, establishment of a permit system to control industrial loading, and installation of online monitoring equipment at point sources are priorities set in the region plan. Moreover, Pollution Control Department is revising effluent standards in order to control and prevent pollution discharged from various point sources more effectively and efficiently.

With regard to domestic wastewater management, a municipal action plan consists of four key measures including wastewater control and minimization at point sources, public participation, effective law enforcement, and rehabilitation and construction of wastewater treatment facilities. Currently, there are nine and three wastewater treatment plants in Chonburi and Rayong provinces, respectively. All of these will be rehabilitated in the near future. A total of 25 wastewater treatment facilities will be constructed in both provinces in order to manage the increasing amount of wastewater. All of the new wastewater treatment plants are to be constructed by 2036 in the priority area to treat all the wastewater generated from point sources (OIC, 2019[10]).

The following sections address the issues identified as a priority by the ONWR within the main two topics, water demand management in the ECC and water and sanitation financing, and provide recommendations based on other countries experience.

It is important to highlight that no quantitative analysis was carried out for the analysis, due to lack of access to the required quantitative data. Therefore, the recommendations provided aim to guide the direction that Thai's authorities might wish to explore to increase water security. However, all recommendations provided in this document should be fine-tuned, reviewed and implemented under an action plan based on more robust data.

## References

Asian Development Bank (2020), *Asian Water Development Outlook 2020*, Asian Development Bank, https://doi.org/10.22617/SGP200412-2. [5]

Chokchai ,, S. and K. Sucharit (2019), "Evaluation of Water Productivity of Thailand and Improvement Measure Proposals", https://www.koreascience.or.kr/article/CFKO201936062693853.pdf. [4]

EEC Office (2019), "EEC Brochure 2019 (EN)". [8]

EEC Policy Committee (2020), *EEC Water Management Plan*, https://www.eeco.or.th/en/news-release-pr/NO-1-2020-The-Eastern-Economic-Corridor-Policy-Committee-1st-issue (accessed on 2022). [9]

OECD (2019), *Multi-dimensional Review of Thailand (Volume 2): In-depth Analysis and Recommendations*, OECD Development Pathways, OECD Publishing, Paris, https://doi.org/10.1787/9789264307674-en. [1]

OIC (2019), "WasteWater Management in EEC". [10]

Petpongpan, C., C. Ekkawatpanit and D. Kositgittiwong (2020), "Climate change impact on surface water and groundwater recharge in northern Thailand", *Water (Switzerland)*, Vol. 12/4, https://doi.org/10.3390/W12041029. [7]

Ta, L. and K. Watershed (2008), *IMPACT OF URBAN EXPANSION ON WATER DEMAND : The case study of Nakhonrachasima city*. [3]

The World Bank Group (2021), *THAILAND CLIMATE RISK COUNTRY PROFILE*, http://www.worldbank.org. [6]

The World Bank Group and the Asian Development Bank (2021), *Climate Risk Country Profile: Thailand*, https://reliefweb.int/sites/reliefweb.int/files/resources/climate-risk-country-profile-thailand.pdf. [2]

## Notes

[1] Resolving problems from the performance of work of State agencies and local government organisations which take action in accordance with the laws, Regulations or Rules binding them insofar as they are concerned with the use, development, management, maintenance, rehabilitation and conservation of water resources, with a view to generating integration as well as public participation (Water Resources Act, 2018).

# 3 Water demand management in the Eastern Economic Corridor

The chapter characterises tensions between rising demand and limited availability of water in the Eastern Economic Corridor. It presents the benefits of a range of measures, which can alleviate these tensions, while mitigating some of the harmful consequences of supply augmentation. Particular attention is paid to the reform of water allocation regimes, the modalities of water transfer from another basin, and the conditions to stimulate demand for reclaimed water in the EEC.

According to the Royal Irrigation Department assessment, by 2037 water demand will increase by 13 percent in the EEC (Table 3.1), with a current annual growth of 27.7 percent. The domestic water sector is the main driver for additional water demand with an estimated growth rate of 56 percent in 20 years, followed by industry with a growth rate estimated of 43 percent. However, agriculture is the sector with the highest total consumption now and in the future, with a growth rate estimated of 17 percent by 2027.

Table 3.1. Water demand projection in the EEC provinces and neighbouring provinces

|  | 2017 | 2027 | Demand increase(Vol) | Demand increase(Rate) |
|---|---|---|---|---|
| Excessive Demand (C=A-B) | 301.3 | 559.48 | 258.2 |  |
| Demand in EEC (A) | 1984.0 | 2242.18 | 258.2 | 13% |
| Chon Buri | 450.0 | 593.25 | 143.3 | 32% |
| Rayong | 592.0 | 650.77 | 58.8 | 10% |
| Chacheingsao | 942.0 | 998.16 | 56.2 | 6% |
| Supply in EEC (B) | 1682.7 | 1682.7 |  |  |
| Chon Buri | 560.9 | 560.9 | Undefined |  |
| Rayong | 643.8 | 643.8 | Undefined |  |
| Chacheingsao | 478.0 | 478.0 | Undefined |  |

Source: Background Information Gathering and Fact Finding on Thailand Water-Related Challenges and Policy Agenda, ONWR, Thailand, 2021

Chon Buri province is and is projected to be the province with the highest volume consumption in absolute terms, but with the lowest increase 12% growth in 2027. Chonburi and Rayong Province are projected to increase their water demand by 50% at least in 2037. Figure 3.1. provides the detail projections for EEC provinces and neighbouring provinces.

Figure 3.1. Water demand projections in the EEC per sector and water source

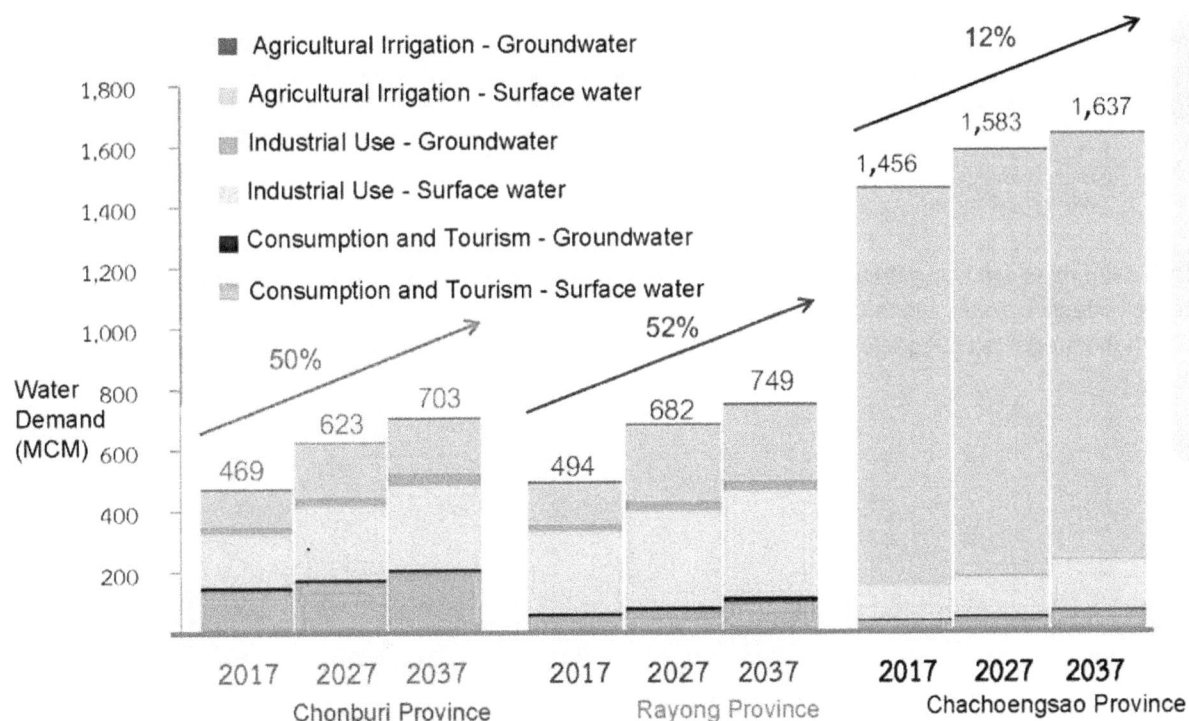

Source: Background Information Gathering and Fact Finding on Thailand Water-Related Challenges and Policy Agenda, ONWR, 2022

**Robust water allocation regimes are required to ensure water security in the region and minimise tensions during scarcity time in the EEC.** According to the preliminary study of water demand and supply in three EEC provinces, it was found that total water supply in the whole Eastern Region was around 2.936 billion cubic metres, while water supply in the three EEC provinces was 1.682 billion cubic metres. However, water demand already overpasses current supply: the demand for water consumption requirement for all economic activities in the entire Eastern Region was 3.833 billion cubic metres, while in the three EEC provinces the demand was 1.984 billion cubic metres (EEC Office, 2019[1]).

**Currently, the magnitude of the potential water insecurity in the EEC does not seem to be fully considered.** Climate change and water resources management risks could threaten water security to new levels which may not be addressed by current water developments in the EEC. According to Water Users groups and key agencies of the Thai government (EEC Secretariat, Royal Irrigation Department and ONWR) the current water development plan is considered sufficient to address future water insecurity in the region, by avoiding future shortage during drought periods. Trust from the civil society can be interpreted as a result of Thai's government commitment to ensure that water supply covers water demand.

International experience suggests that such a statement may need to be qualified. First, supply augmentation comes at increasing social, environmental, economic and financial costs. Additional infrastructure needs to be built, and then operated and maintained, creating future liabilities. This is particularly an issue when future water demand and availability are uncertain (be it only because of climate change). In addition to finance, economic costs derive from the fact that additional water capacity may not contribute to water use efficiency. Environmental costs can be complex, when sediments are stopped from flowing because of dams, environmental flows are not sustained when too much water is abstracted from water bodies, or when additional (fossil) energy is used to augment supply. Social costs occur when the costs of augmenting supply are unevenly allocated across user groups and communities. Second, a combination of demand management and supply augmentation can be more robust in the face of uncertainties about future water availability and demand. Third, such a combination can be cost-effective, when all the costs sketched above are considered; it can result is less pressure on scarce public finance (see OECD, 2013; OECD, 2021). Water allocation regimes can go a long way managing water demand - from existing and new users. They can allocate water where it creates most value to communities (OECD, 2015).

## 3.1. State of play of water allocation in the EEC

Thai authorities are committed to ensuring that water allocation regimes (Box 3.1) are fit for the future and deliver effective water allocation under normal conditions and in times of water scarcity. The background information received suggests that responses to scarcity in Thailand translate into limiting or banning some uses.

Box 3.1. Water Allocation Regimes in Thailand

Thailand's Water Resources Act (2018) stipulates clauses on water allocation for the best use of limited water resources in terms of economic necessity, efficiency and equity. According to the Section 41 of the Act, the use of Public Water Resources is classified into three types: domestic use including household and agricultural use, industrial use including power generation, and irrigation. Those who want to use water for industrial and irrigation purposes have to hold legitimate rights including approval from Director Generals of Royal Irrigation Department, Department of Water Resources and Department of Groundwater Resources.

A Water Abstraction Charge is applied to surface water and ground water for promoting water saving behaviour. However, the abstraction charge rate does not reflect seasonal scarcity and remains stable throughout the year.

Source: 1) Questionnaire for the National Dialogue on Water in Thailand, ONWR, Thailand, 2021
2) Background Information Gathering and Fact Finding on Thailand Water-Related Challenges and Policy Agenda, ONWR, Thailand, 2021
3) Cities and Flooding, A Guide to Integrated Urban Flood Risk Management for the 21st Century, World Bank, 2011

The Water Resources Act 2018 divides water users in three categories, without clearly quantifying the distinctions between them:

1. Type 1: the use of public water resources for the living, household consumption, agriculture or livestock farming for subsistence, household industry, ecosystem conservation, customs, public disaster mitigation, communications and the use of water in a small quantity;
2. Type 2: the use of public water resources for the industry, tourism industry, electricity generation, waterworks and other undertakings;
3. Type 3: the use of public water resources for a large-sized undertaking which requires the use of a large quantity of water or possibly has effects across drainage basins or covering large areas

The water use of Type 1 "requires no water use licence and is subject to no payment of fees", regardless of the farming surface. Taking into account that irrigated agriculture is the major consumer of water resources in the EEC, users Type 1 consume up to 65% of the total volume in some provinces (Table 3.2.), it can be a critical element to limit water security in the EEC and the country.

Table 3.2. Water demand in the EEC's provinces

| EEC province code | Consumption – all type users (MCM) | | Industry – all type users (MCM) | | Agriculture – Type 1 (MCM) | | Total | Water demand in Eastern Region |
|---|---|---|---|---|---|---|---|---|
| 2560 | 251 | 10.38% | 606 | 25.05% | 1562 | 64.57% | 2419 | 4167 |
| 2570 | 309 | 10.70% | 748 | 25.90% | 1831 | 63.40% | 2888 | 5481 |
| 2580 | 392 | 12.69% | 865 | 28.00% | 1832 | 59.31% | 3089 | 5775 |

Source: Background Information Gathering and Fact Finding on Thailand Water-Related Challenges and Policy Agenda, ONWR, Thailand, 2022

Currently, water allocation in the EEC is assessed through two situations. During normal situation, the River Basin Committee is responsible for considering water usage, water allocation, prioritizing water usage in each river basin activity, and controlling the use of water in accordance with the framework of rules and guidelines prescribed by the National Water Resources Committee (NWRC), including the Eastern Economic Corridor Committee. To increase water security, a plan is prepared in advance by the River Basin Committee to prevent and resolve drought and flood situations. It is approved by NWRC and submitted to the governor, government agencies, and local government organizations. However, the River Basin Committee does not have a mechanism for analysing and forecasting the water situation.

During extreme events, defined as "an event of a water crisis that may affect the livelihoods of people, animals, plants, or may cause severe damage to the property of the people or the state", the Prime Minister establishes an Ad Hoc Command Centre to manage the crisis until it returns to normal. During this period, the National Water Command (NWC) act as a secretary in conducting monitoring, surveillance, analysis, pointing out the risk areas and adjusting the plan. Measures set up include limiting and banning some activities, which affects farmers and industry.

Such command-and-control responses are common globally. However, they can trigger equity issues and can unduly affect economic development. In particular, they can lead to unfair and inefficient allocation of risks across water users in the basin. Typically, they disproportionally affect low value uses and provide no incentives for other uses to enhance water use efficiency. Other options could be considered, thanks to robust water allocation regimes.

Given the inherent variability of water resources and shifting pressures and social preferences, in particular with the important transformation happening in the EEC, water allocation regimes need to be both robust and demonstrate adaptive capacity. This requires striking a balance between the need for flexibility at the system level and security at the user level, giving both water managers and water users' greater capacity to manage risk. The following section presents recommendations on water allocation regimes, water demand management as well as compensation mechanisms for inter-basins water transfers in the EEC.

## 3.2. Recommendations on water allocation regimes

### 3.2.1. Strengthen system and user level elements of the water allocation regime

**The EEC, River Basin Committees will benefit from assessing the robustness of their water allocation regime at system and user level.** The complex and distinctive features of water resources as an economic good and its particular legal status mean that allocation regimes are often complex combinations of various laws, policies, and mechanisms. The robustness and adaptive efficiency of an allocation regime can be improved by unbundling the various elements and using separate instruments to pursue various objectives. However, unbundling should not undermine the effective management of the system as a whole. Therefore, even if separate instruments are used to achieve particular objectives, there is still a need for a comprehensive view of how the various elements interact. The elements of an allocation regime can be divided into "system level" and "user level" elements (OECD, 2015[2]).

System level elements are those that are most efficiently and equitably dealt with at the scale of the water body, whether it is the basin, catchment, river, stream or aquifer. They range from identifying the availability of water resources, to the legal status of the resource, to mechanisms for monitoring and enforcement, see Table 3.3 (OECD, 2015[2]).

## Table 3.3. Description of key system level elements of a water allocation regime

| System level elements | Description |
|---|---|
| Legal status of the ownership of water resources | Legal definition of the ownership of water resources (e.g. public, private, res nullius). |
| Institutional arrangements for allocation | Authorities and organisations responsible for allocation and their various roles (policy, planning, issuing entitlements, monitoring and enforcement) |
| Identification of available water resources | Identification of available water resources (surface, ground water as well as treated waste water intended for re-use) based on best available scientific evidence. |
| Identification of in situ flow requirements / available ("allocable") resource pool | An explicit definition of in situ flow requirements based on various factors, such as requirements for base flow, environmental flows, non-consumptive use, international commitments, inter-annual and intra-annual variability, and climate change. The remaining water would be considered the available resource pool |
| Abstraction limit ("cap") | An explicit and enforceable limit on abstraction. It may be defined in absolute, volumetric terms or as a proportion of available resources. The "cap" can be used to ensure water for environmental needs, so it should be designed to reflect natural flow regime dynamics. |
| Definition of permitted uses not required to hold an entitlement | Definition of those water users and uses that are allowed to access and use water without holding an entitlement |
| Definition of "exceptional circumstances" | An explicit definition of circumstances that are considered "exceptional" and may require extraordinary measures. Stakeholders may or may not be involved in the definition of what constitutes "exceptional circumstances" |
| Sequence of priority uses | A pre-defined sequence of priority uses sets out the priority of access to water according to types of uses or users. It may apply when "exceptional circumstances" are declared or be used to guide the allocation of water entitlements |
| Requirements for new entrants or expanded water entitlements | Conditions placed on the acquisition of new water entitlements or requests to expand existing entitlements. Typical examples include the assessment of third party impacts, environmental impact assessments or existing users foregoing use (for instance, in situations where the catchment is closed). |
| Mechanisms for monitoring and enforcement | Mechanisms such as metering, aerial surveillance or other means of monitoring water abstraction and use as well as clearly defined procedures and sanctions for addressing infractions and resolving conflicts. |
| Appropriate infrastructures | Water infrastructures to allow water to be stored, treated and transported, as needed |

Source: OECD (2015), Water Resources Allocation: Sharing Risks and Opportunities, OECD Studies on Water, OECD Publishing, Paris. http://dx.doi.org/10.1787/9789264229631-en.

In the EEC, River Basin Committees may need to reinforce some elements of the water allocation regime, in particular the demand side such as identification of *in situ* flow requirements, abstraction limit and requirements for new entrants. Demand based water policies are considered most cost efficient and sustainable in the long term (OECD, 2016[3]).

Thai authorities, through their ambitious reforms of the water sector, are addressing numerous system elements such as providing appropriate infrastructures, the legal status, the institutional arrangement and definition of exception circumstances.

In addition, water security in the EEC would benefit from having a more accurate supply assessment under extreme events, which could set more realistic limits to water abstraction and access to new entrants, to be able to increase water resilience. Thai government has already started to reinforce this element by developing "One Map", a "national data bank on water and climate" as a database gathering real time information from related agencies, grouping information on rain, rain and storm forecast, flood water, level of water in different sources, such as reservoirs, large natural water sources, and main rivers; as well as water quality and emergency area (ONWR, 2019[4]).

Data gathering and homogenisation are key elements to support more accurate water allocation regimes. However, they are not sufficient. Decision making processes need to be established, including threshold for water abstraction during normal times and dry periods, application of these thresholds through policy, economic and regulatory instruments and thresholds revision to adapt to changing conditions. For example, without having a realistic cap for water abstraction in the basin, regardless of the data precision, very limited effective measures can be implemented to address future water insecurity in the EEC.

User level elements of a water allocation regime are those aspects that are most efficiently and equitably dealt with by specifying the arrangements that apply to an individual (or collective) abstractor. Typically, these take the form of arrangements specified in entitlements, permits and licenses.

Table 3.4. Description of key user level elements of a water allocation regime

| User level elements | Description |
| --- | --- |
| Legal definition of water entitlements | A legal definition of water entitlements that confers the right to use the resource, usually under certain conditions as well as identification of the types of water users that are required to hold an entitlement in order to abstract water. Entitlements may or may not be privately held. They can be granted to individuals or to collective bodies, such as water users' associations. The definition usually also determines how an entitlement can be withheld or cancelled. |
| Abstraction charges | Charges associated with water abstraction. They aim to recover costs and to internalise negative externalities associated with water abstractions. As a proxy, most charges are set administratively and are designed to recover the costs associated with water supply provision. |
| Obligations relating to return flows in water entitlements | Return flow obligations refer to the requirement to return a portion of the water abstracted to the same or a different water body following use. Discharge requirements relate to the quality requirements (including thermal changes) of discharges. |
| Duration for water entitlements, and expectations for renewal | The length of time a water entitlement is granted for. It may be for a given number of years or in perpetuity (often conditional on beneficial use). |
| Possibility to trade, lease or transfer | The ability for water entitlement holders to trade (either permanently or temporarily), lease or transfer entitlements to others. |

Source: OECD (2015), Water Resources Allocation: Sharing Risks and Opportunities, OECD Studies on Water, OECD Publishing, Paris. http://dx.doi.org/10.1787/9789264229631-en

Several measures at user level could make water allocation more robust in the EEC. Licenses and related abstraction charges could be set up for water use of Type 1 which benefit from water services delivery. This could be done at a group level to be most cost-effective. Even if individually the volume consumed is small for Type 1 users, the total volume consumed by all Type 1 users is the highest (Table 3.2.). France has explored options to regulate water abstraction from groups of small users. It does so through collective entitlements to abstract water, which are then managed by water user associations without further interference from any regulating agency. Box 3.2 illustrates the French case.

Providing clearer guidelines on what is meant by "small quantity" for water uses from Type 1 would strengthen water allocation, as well.

Without setting in place licences for all users or some form of cap on how much water can be abstracted (individually or collectively), water security could be compromised now and in the future, regardless of how much additional water can be supplied. Licences, and the economic instruments linked to them, are key tools to ensure water security in the region. By leaving the biggest number of users and the highest cumulative water consumption outside the water allocation regime and any regulation about water abstraction, the EEC region as well as the whole country could be jeopardising its water security.

## Box 3.2. Collective water entitlements, a solution to regulate numerous small water users

In France, water is generally abundant, although water stress is increasing in some regions and there are periodic episodes of scarcity. Ground and surface water are designated as part of the "Common Heritage of the Nation". Recent reforms include changes in abstraction volumes (to match available water with the needs of users) and the creation of Single Collective Management Bodies (Organismes Uniques de Gestion Collective, OUGC) for small-scale irrigation. OUGCs are an institutional arrangement to manage a collective entitlement to abstract water from a catchment.

The rationale is that basin agencies do not have the capacity to monitor water abstraction from multiple farmers in a catchment, and to enforce compliance with water entitlements. In that context, water agencies offer to grant a collective entitlement to abstract water to a group of water uses in the catchment. Such a group is called OUGC. The group is then tasked with the management of that collective entitlement, in effect allocating water among its constituency in a fair and equitable way. Basin agencies do not interfere further with OUGCs, as long as OUGCs can demonstrate they operate in an un-biased way

This provides a lot of flexibility for OUGCs to deal with the specific requirements of individual farmers (depending on the crop they grow, their farming practices, etc.) without direct supervision from the regulator, while contributing to a robust water allocation regime.

However, some challenges emerged with the implementation of collective water entitlements and the operation of OUGCs. Conflictual relations have risen between the OUGCs and irrigators; in some instances, decision-making procedures may have restrained the influence of some stakeholders. Furthermore, some farmers have reacted to the fact that their individual, permanent water entitlements would be replaced by collective ones. Also, a lack of clarity regarding key aspects in the legislation, including with regards to sanctioning and the judicial relation between the OUGC and the farmers, has led to further lack of support of the collective management model.

With adjustment to reflect local conditions, this model could be considered in the EEC (and in other parts of the country). The management of collective water entitlements can be carried out by a number of different groups or institutions, including agricultural chambers, groups of local irrigators, owners of land used for irrigation, local legal groups or territorial associations.

In France, those wishing to operate an OUGC apply to the Prefecture (local representative of the state), which appoints the most suitable group in collaboration with the local Water Agency and agricultural chamber. The majority of existing OUGCs are run by agricultural chambers, while a few are operated by irrigators' unions. The body appointed as OUGC is initially given a time-bound mandate (three to five years), with the possibility of extension for an unlimited period of time. It is in charge of collecting water withdrawal requests from irrigators in the catchment, and, based on these requests, proposes annual plans for the allocation of its collective entitlement. The Prefecture determines the collective entitlement for agriculture in that catchment, based on a nationally-defined minimum water flow. In addition, the OUGC develop multi-annual plans projecting the apportionment of the water entitlement for irrigation over a period of up to 15 years. Annual and multi-annual plans are endorsed by the Prefecture, with or without amendments. It is important to note that the mission of the OUGC is only to prepare the decisions of the Prefecture, which remains the ultimate authority with regards to water allocation.

Source: OECD (2017), Groundwater Allocation: Managing Growing Pressures on Quantity and Quality, OECD Studies on Water, OECD Publishing, Paris. http://dx.doi.org/10.1787/9789264281554-en

### 3.2.2. E-flow management to preserve the resource

Environmental flows refer to the quantity, quality and timing of water flows required to sustain the ecological health of a water body. More precisely, Thailand defines minimum environmental flow as "the flow with 90% exceeding of duration (Q90) to sustain the ecological health of waterway" (ONWR, 2019[4]). Thai authorities estimate that 27,090 billion cubic meters are required to preserve ecosystem during droughts in the country (ONWR, 2019[4]).

Thai authorities would benefit from reinforcing environmental flows in the EEC, in particular developing policies ensuring protection under the secondary laws under the Act on Water Resources Management. The Water Resources Act does not mention explicitly environmental flow, which may limit environmental flows legitimacy to be considered as part of the allocation process. Having in place a methodology to set minimum environmental flows does not ensure its application. Its absence in the Act may lead to impunity towards its consideration. The penalties in the Act currently occur once the damage has taken place (section 85) which limits the options to protect the resource and increases the costs in the long term. In relation to environmental water, the Act only sets the conservation and development of public water resources by identifying the areas (water sources, creek and wetlands) and identifying the criteria for making use of land that may affect public water resources. These two elements are key to protect the resources but may not be sufficient to ensure its protection in the long term. Pillar 1 of the Master Plan on Water Resource Management "*hold the principle of balance in conservation, rehabilitation and development of water sources*" (ONWR, 2019[4]) needs to be applied.

Freshwater systems provide a wide range of ecosystem services, and those services depend on particular flow regimes. This includes many services beyond traditional "conservation" objectives, and can include services such as flood attenuation or the provision of water for human consumption. Failure to provide adequate environmental flows can lead to a wide range of negative, and often unexpected, impacts. International experience shows it is extremely difficult to recover water for the environment once it has been allocated for consumptive use. This highlights the importance of reserving appropriate flows for environmental purposes from the outset (OECD, 2015[5]).

It does not follow from the considerations above that environment should be given priority vis-à-vis other water uses in the EEC. The point is that due consideration should be given to the needs of the environment (in particular, freshwater ecosystems) from the outset and the likely consequences of reductions or other changes to instream flows: understanding how much water ecosystems need to provide the services on which our well-being relies is a requisite to factor the environment in allocation decisions. Underestimating these needs can be very costly in the end (either because ecosystems may fail to function or because their protection or restoration will be more costly at a later date); overestimating them results in lost opportunities for other valuable purposes. (OECD, 2015[5]).

During water scarcity time at the EEC, addressing return flows can be particularly challenging, because entitlement holders have an incentive to reduce return flows and save the water for themselves. This can undermine the integrity of the allocation regime if the change in the effective rate of consumption is not accounted for. There are generally two approaches to address this issue:

    i)    reducing the abstraction limit as the technical efficiency of water use increases, with the reduction averaged across all entitlement holders equally; or

    ii)    Specifying return flow obligations in water entitlements.

Choosing between these options depends on an assessment of administrative costs and preference for stimulating innovation in the EEC. The first approach rewards first movers in the pursuit of technically more efficient uses of water. The rate of adoption of more efficient irrigation technology should be faster. Those that move first, benefit from access to water that was previously being used by others. The latter approach is more equitable, as changes in the choice of technology made by one person, which increase the technical efficiency of water use, have no impact on the amount of water allocated to all other users, as would be the case in the first approach. However, the latter approach is much more expensive to administer as the type of technology used by each person needs to be tracked and accounted for (OECD, 2015[5]).

In some cases, including several parts of the United States, a hybrid approach is taken. No attempt is made to account for changes within a farm, but when an entitlement is transferred to another person the entitlement is adjusted for expected changes in the return flow (OECD, 2015[2]).

## 3.3. Recommendations on complementary measures to manage water demand

Water allocation regimes can only be effective when combined with pricing and non-pricing measures across sectors. Demand side approaches offer multiple benefits compared to supply-side approaches. These include reduced costs from reduced water treatment and energy use (e.g. treatment, heating); savings in capital expenditures through downsized new supply projects; and increased environmental benefits of reduced withdrawals. At the same time, water demand management requires a high level of expertise, knowledge and know-how, together with capital (upfront) investments, for example, the installation of water meters or the replacement of distribution networks. Based on other countries experience, the efficiency and effectiveness of particular non-price and price measures depend on several dimensions, such as the level of water scarcity, level of awareness, institutional context or the quality of the infrastructure (European Environmental Agency, 2017[6]).

### 3.3.1. Non-pricing mechanism to reduce water consumption

Restrictions of water supply in times of acute water scarcity are generally considered to be effective in reducing the water demand in the short term. However, they have no or marginal effect on water demand in the long term if they are not accompanied by other measures such as leakage reduction, water saving devices and awareness campaigns (European Environmental Agency, 2017[6]).

Thai authorities could benefit from reinforcing non-pricing measures under EEC water allocation regimes. However, these measures would need to be combined with pricing measures to reach their maximum potential.

One of the key challenges of non-pricing mechanisms, in particular in times of restricted public finance, is that they often require financial resources for their implementation. This is the case for subsidies for the installation of water saving devices and for consumer awareness campaigns – even though the implementation costs of awareness campaigns are relatively low as compared to many other (infrastructure-like) measures.

### 3.3.2. Network leakage reduction

EEC authorities would benefit from reinforcing the water demand side management long term plan by reducing water losses, reducing network leakage across all sectors.

Under the EEC water management plan, network leakage reduction or reducing water losses are key elements to manage demand in collaboration with the Provincial Waterworks Authority and the Industrial sector. Leakage in the distribution networks is not compatible with the increasing trend towards sustainability, economic efficiency and environmental protection. Water losses are an inevitable part of the practice of public water supply, which from a resource efficiency perspective should be minimised. The term includes production losses and distribution losses, which again includes real losses in the network and unbilled consumption (European Environmental Agency, 2017[6]).

Thai authorities would need to take into account that investments needed for improved leakage efficiency must compete with other priorities for operating and capital funds, and must be based on a sound financial case of costs and benefits. To reduce water losses, Provincial Waterworks Authority could measure the volume of lost water by water service providers. It is important to note that water services providers often offer the position that they are operating as efficiently as they can, given their specific circumstances, and that further increases in efficiency to reduce leakage would require increased tariffs, which can be politically unpopular.

In the EEC, effective reduction in leakage can become more complex with increasing water shortages and potential reduction in consumption in the long term. When a distribution system faces shortage, the last resort is to stop distributing water for parts to allow some replenishment of the reserves. "Stop and go" is socially harmful and potentially unfair. Moreover, it affects the infrastructure through brutal changes in the pressure in the network. This is why a thorough leakage reduction programme is preferable.

### 3.3.3. Water use efficiency in the agriculture sector

To ensure water security in the EEC, Thai authorities would benefit from exploring water use efficiency for the agricultural sector. According to the Royal Irrigation Department, the current strategy of the for water management is to increase supply by building water storage facilities to support farmers.

Other countries, facing similar water scarcity challenges, have put strong emphasis on water use efficiency as a means to reduce structural water stress and vulnerability to the risk of water shortage. Water use efficiency has different components: distribution, application and retention. Different technical options are potentially available to improve water use efficiency which would allow the agricultural sector to produce more while also freeing up water resources for other users and uses.

While improving water use efficiency is necessary to move forward a green growth strategy in agriculture, several issues must be addressed to ensure that policy approaches achieve their objectives. A too narrow focus on water use efficiency, together with a lack of water policy coherence could lead to perverse effects and counterproductive outcomes (OECD, 2016[3]). Three issues are of particular concern in this area:

- Hydrological paradox. When assessing water efficiency, return flows tend to be ignored. Water use efficiency measures tend to reduce return flows, resulting in less water being available for users downstream (including for environmental purposes), thereby exacerbating scarcity. This is a major error and can lead to environmental risks at the catchment level. Mitigating these unintended consequences of water use efficiency gains requires appropriate water accounting at the basin scale that considers not just withdrawals but also water returning to the system. Moving from hydrological science to the inclusion of such return flows in water right systems is, however, a complex task. Accounting for return flows should thus be studied more systemically to assess their relative importance in watersheds. And return flows would need to be accounted for in water allocation (OECD, 2016[3]).
- Risk of rebound effect. Water use efficiency frees water, which becomes available to expand irrigated land. This happens when water savings arising from efficiency gains are captured by the farmer, rather than returned to the water system. As a consequence, water use efficiency can lead to extension of irrigated surfaces, not to more water being available for users downstream (including the environment). The classical corollary is that water use efficiency gains should be accompanied by a regulation of water demand or irrigated surfaces to prevent this rebound effect from occurring (OECD, 2016[3]).
- Indirect impact associated with production choices. Even taking into account the previous risks of perverse effects, investments to increase water use efficiency can incite farmers to follow a path of specialisation in irrigated crops, which in the end would make them more dependent on water resources and the risks associated with climate change (OECD, 2016[3]).

## 3.4. Recommendations on compensation measures

### 3.4.1. Water transfer compensation measures

The current water management plan in the EEC includes water diversion. This can exacerbate growing competition across riparian regions (providers versus receivers of water).

Robust allocation regimes can minimise equity issues related to such a competition. Still, compensation measures may be required. As suggested earlier, the reform of water allocation regimes could provide ample opportunities for participation and negotiation. Thai authorities' willingness to engage stakeholders and appropriately compensate potential "losers" facilitates the process. Compensations can take various forms, such as funding to build storage structures in some EEC provinces (Chachoengsao) and neighbouring provinces (Chanthaburi) providing water. Regardless of the compensation measure selected, minimising equity issues and designing fair and cost-effective compensation are key.

Many countries with similar socio-economic (developing regions with high tourism and industry and wealth inequality) and hydro-climatic conditions (semi-arid versus abundant water regions) have put in place inter-basins transfers. They do not include compensation measures; at places receiving bodies pay for the volume transferred (on the basis of some bulk water tariff). Most inter-basins transfers are based on the principle of solidarity between wealthier and water abundant regions and poorer and water scarce regions within a country. Box 3.3 provides details on the Brazilian experience with the São Francisco Integration Project water transfer.

## Box 3.3. Brazilian São Francisco Integration water transfer project

In Brazil, due to its economic and hydrological characteristics, the Piancó-Piranhas Açu (PPA) River Basin is fragile in terms of securing present and future water supply. The basin's hydro-climatology is characterised by an absence of rain during most of the year, combined with multi-year drought periods that occur periodically. From 2012 to 2020, the basin experienced one of its worst periods of severe multi-year drought (de Sousa Freitas, 2021[7]). Most rivers are intermittent, thus almost all water supply is provided by reservoirs. Some of these reservoirs operate to maintain river flow and serve as a source of water for irrigators, public water supply and others. PPA is home to 29% of the Brazilian population but only have 3.3% of the country's water resources.

Despite the reservoirs, 60% (31 out of 52) of the hydrological planning units in the Piancó-Piranhas Açu River Basin have a negative water supply/demand balance (ANA, 2016[8]). The water resource of the basin aquifers is limited (annual recharge of 458 hm$^3$, equivalent to 8% of the water stored in reservoirs) and little used (93 hm$^3$ or 20% of the annual recharge). Irrigation accounts for two thirds of water demand, fish farming 22%, public water supply 7%, industry and livestock share the remaining 4% (ANA, 2016[8]). There is a lack of investment in water security (e.g. dams, reservoirs, wastewater collection and treatment), due to the limited capacity to invest in the basin. Therefore, targeted measures are needed to enhance the basin's resilience, cope with supply and pollution issues, and competition across water users.

The São Francisco River transfer, known as the São Francisco Integration Project (PISF), will reduce uncertainty over water availability in the Piancó-Piranhas Açu River Basin. In 2007, Brazil launched the PISF and began building infrastructure to boost economic development in the northeast of the country, including the PPA basin. The PISF is the most expensive Brazilian hydraulic infrastructure to date, expected to reach BRL 12 billion (USD 5.8 billion) (da Silva Santos, 2021[9]). Originally scheduled for completion by 2011, the project experienced several delays and cost overruns. Currently in the final phase of execution, the project aims to divert 1.4% of the largest river located exclusively in Brazil to the semi-arid zones of north-eastern Brazil. It also aims to help the Northeast hydraulic network operate in a more synergistic way (hence the reference in the project name to integration rather than diversion). The project is implemented by the Ministry of Regional Development. The transfer is supposed to enhance the economic development of the region, by ensuring supply for all users in the Basin.

The first phase of the PISF is now in place and starting to highlight issues relating to the operation and maintenance of major water infrastructure. The federal government was responsible for financing and delivering the construction phase, establishing the management system and defining the operator at federal level. The States are responsible for operation and maintenance and water use. However, no clear financial strategy is in place to cover the operation and maintenance costs, requiring the institutional development of government agencies, river basin organisms and operational institutions responsible for hydrologic monitoring, water use control and reservoir operations.

No compensation mechanism was established for the inter-basin transfer. Water users should pay for the water received. States would charge beneficiaries and provide funds for the operator. Under a contractual arrangement, state water agencies in both States should pay the PISF federal operator to receive bulk water from it. However, there is no legal provision allowing water agencies to recover these costs from end users. In Brazil, for federal reservoirs, the federal government fully supports operation and maintenance costs. For PISF, energy costs are a major operational expense. They vary over the year, making tariff setting very challenging.

Source: OECD (2022), Fostering Water Resilience in Brazil: Turning Strategy into Action, OECD Studies on Water, OECD Publishing, Paris, https://doi.org/10.1787/85a99a7c-en

In a different context, Korea has set up a mechanism to compensate territories and communities upstream of a river for the distinctive constrains they face to protect water quality to the benefits of users downstream. This financial transfer mechanisms is designed to compensate for the impacts such constraints have on the capacity of these communities to grow and develop. Although it is designed to manage water quality, this mechanism can be a source of inspiration for Thai authorities when considering a financial mechanism to compensate basins which agree to share their waters with other basins.

---

Box 3.4. River Management Funds for water quality improvement of Korea's major river basins

To improve the water quality of the four major river basins, the ME set up water use charges to fund projects that would reduce water pollution in upstream areas. Based on the User-Pays Principle, the water use charges collect revenue from downstream users (cities and industries) to offset the losses in opportunity costs to upstream users associated with regulations against various economic activities.

Water use charges apply to downstream households, commercial entities and industry in proportion to the volume of water received and used. Water use charge rates are determined every two years based on forecasted financial resources required to achieve the target level of water quality pursuant to the law. As of 2016, the water use charge rates were KRW 170/ton for the Han, Nakdong and Yeongsan-Seomjin Rivers, and KRW 160/ton for the Geum River.

The revenue from the water use charges enters River Management Funds (RMFs). Water use charges and the RMF were first introduced in 1999 for the Han River, followed by the other major river basins in 2002. In 2015, the RMFs raised a total of KRW 10.14 trillion.

The RMF spend is overseen by the River Basin Committee in each basin, which aims to coordinate the interests of diverse stakeholders on matters relating to water quality improvements. The RMFs supports two main activity areas: i) catchment restoration and protection activities, and ii) wastewater infrastructure. Types of projects include:

- Sewage treatment infrastructure, matching the subsidy funds from national government, and subsidising operational costs (48% of total RMF spend)
- Resident support: income support, low interest rate loans, compensation (18% of total RMF spend)
- Voluntary land purchase and riparian zone projects (transformation and management of acquired land) (18% of total RMF spend). As of 2016, farmers have offered 156 million m2 of land for purchase, but only 60 million m2 has been purchased because of funding constraints. The total area of 'designated riparian zones' reached 1197 km2 as of 2015.
- Total pollutant load control, through subsidies to local government to work on pollution management, monitoring and research (5% of total RMF spend).
- Other water quality improvement projects, including removing litter, monitoring programmes by NGOs, subsidising water treatment from polluted water resources, dredging, public education and ecosystem restoration (8% of total RMF spend).

Source: OECD (2018), Managing the Water-Energy-Land-Food Nexus in Korea: Policies and Governance Options, OECD Studies on Water, OECD Publishing, Paris, https://doi.org/10.1787/9789264306523-en.

---

Several elements should be considered when putting in place inter-basins transfers which include compensation measures between regions:

- Economic analysis is required to evaluate if the net regional income gain due to the transfer in the EEC is positive, given all feasible alternatives to the transfer, including the equivalent value of environmental changes. From an economic perspective, a transfer should occur if the transferred water, including the costs of transportation and payment for third-party income losses and environmental costs, is the least cost water available to the importing basin. These considerations normally demonstrate how cost-effective water demand management is, compared to inter-basin transfers.

- The water price for the water transferred should aim to recover the full cost of the resource (the financial cost of building and operating the infrastructure, and the opportunity cost of adding constraints to water users in the source basin). It should not only consider operation and maintenance costs, it should include environmental and social costs as well. As illustrated by the Spanish case (Box 3.4), inter-basin water transfers raise the cost of supply significantly and can have substantial environmental impacts.

---

### Box 3.5. Spanish large water transfer scheme

The Tagus-Segura transfer is a scheme linking the Bolarque Reservoir on the Tagus River in central Spain with the Talave Reservoir on the Segura River in the dry southeast of the country. It is 292 km long and capable of transferring up to 33 m³/s. Its design was based upon the river flow series from 1958-79, which suggested that up to 1,000 hm³/annum was feasible. However, since 1979 flows in the donor basin have declined by 47% and the volume thought to be available for transfer was reduced to 600 hm³/a. In practice, transfers have averaged only 351 hm³/a. One third of the water is used for public supply and the remainder for irrigation. Evaporation and other losses account for about 20 hm³/a.

Despite its economic benefits in the Segura basin, the transfer resulted in significant adverse impacts in both donor and recipient basins. In the Tagus, there were major changes in the river dynamics, increased erosion and reduction of water quality. This deterioration sparked social and political concern. The Segura ecosystems were impacted by the introduction of non-native species of fish, which are dominating local fish populations. In addition, the increase in irrigation caused groundwater levels to rise and become increasingly polluted by nutrients. These impacts led to discussions about how best to manage large transfers, and the need for continuous adaptation.

This experience provides some useful lessons transferable to Thailand:

- Feasibility should be tested under different rainfall and socio-economic scenarios.
- Transfers can create a range of impacts in the affected basins, which should be identified as part of the environmental assessment for the scheme. If they materialise after construction and during operation, they must be addressed and minimised.
- Transfers are very sensitive to climatic change and shifts in social dynamics.
- Effective inter-administrative cooperation is key for sustainable operation of the transfer

Source OECD (2022), Fostering Water Resilience in Brazil: Turning Strategy into Action, OECD Studies on Water, OECD Publishing, Paris, https://doi.org/10.1787/85a99a7c-en

---

As explored by the Thai government, the compensation mechanism could finance additional infrastructures in the origin basin. The receiving basin, as a potential condition of the transfer, could refund the income foregone (including the equivalent value of lost nature) in the basin of origin. Analysis of the potential income losses in the region that shares its water should be assessed taking into account all sectors (agriculture, environment, water supply, industry, energy, among others). The following economic instruments could be explored:

- The receiving basins in the EEC could share the net regional income gain with the basin of origin, through a tax over benefitting sectors. Access to water supply provides spill-over effects for the economy, such as in the EEC area benefitting from infrastructure, industry and tourism development. In addition, it has the potential to attract private businesses to the region, resulting in higher regional income. This, in turn, will bring employment to the region, increasing consumption and demand for other sectors such as housing (OECD/ADBI/Mekong Institute, 2020[10]).

- The tax revenues could be distributed to investors who finance the infrastructure in the origin basin without decreasing existing tax revenues of local and central governments. Returning spill-over tax revenues to investors would encourage the development of rural regions. For example, in the Philippines, the central government finances much of the infrastructure development. If local governments return a part of their increased spill-over tax revenues to the central government, the central government can invest those returned tax revenues into other projects to help mitigate poverty in rural regions (OECD/ADBI/Mekong Institute, 2020[10]).

Water charges in the receiving basins in the EEC could be used to finance compensation measures under specific conditions. According to section 49 (1) of the Water Resources Act 2018, water charges are applicable to users Type 2 and 3. Water tariffs and water charges are two different economic instruments. The first aims to recover the costs of water supply services (building, operating and maintaining the infrastructure; it accrues to the service provider). The latter aims to manage water resources; it reflects the scarcity of the resource (the charge is higher when water is scarce); revenues from the tax can be transferred to the general budget (the preferred option from a public finance perspective), or earmarked for water expenditures (the preferred option from a water policy perspective).

OECD Council Recommendation on Water advises that "setting abstraction charges for surface and ground water that reflect water scarcity (i.e. environmental and resource cost) and that cover administrative costs of managing the system" and "setting water pollution charges for surface and groundwater use and pollution or charges for wastewater discharge at a sufficient level to have a significant incentive effect to prevent and control pollution" (OECD, 2021[11]).

A portion of the water charge could be used to finance infrastructures. This could be justified if the public benefits of infrastructures are established. In the meantime, the absence of sufficient charges in the EEC basin seriously compromises the financing of the river basin plan (assuming implementation of the water pays for water principle). This discussion is currently undergoing in other countries experiencing similar situations as Thailand, such as in the Piancó-Piranhas Açu River Basin in Brazil (OECD, 2022[12]), see Box 3.5.

The charge rate should not vary according to the category of user, as is often the case in OECD countries, where farmers - and sometimes industry - benefit from preferential rates. The water conservation signal would be more effective if the same rate applies for all abstractors. To address affordability issues, two steps should be considered. First, affordability issues should be thoroughly documented and the communities affected clearly identified. Too generic assessments tend to overstate affordability issues, leading to compensation measures that are poorly targeted and benefit users who could afford to pay more. Second, an additional levy on rich abstractors could be collected and redistributed in the basin as income for the poorest to help them pay the rate (cross-subsidy between abstractors). The support would be even more effective if it was earmarked to support transition away from water-intensive practices (e.g. support to new crops, innovative farming techniques, more efficient irrigation schemes). Box 3.6 provides an overview of the functioning of abstraction charges in France (OECD, 2022[12]), which have proven effective as a financing mechanism for water-related expenditures.

## Box 3.6. Water abstraction charges in France

Water abstraction charges were introduced in France in 1964, when the six Water Agencies were created. Revenue from charges is collected by each agency and redistributed in the same basin for investments to protect and improve water resources. The charge must be paid by all those who abstract water above a threshold set by each agency (which cannot be more than 10 000 m³ per year, or 7 000 m³ in areas with water scarcity). Abstraction at sea, aquaculture-related abstractions, and abstractions outside the low-water period and intended for the restoration of natural areas are exempt. Similarly, users who release wastewater pay a pollution charge at basin level, designed to compensate for the cost of mitigating that pollution.

Water Agencies grant subsidies to water users (farmers, municipalities and industries) funded by revenues from abstraction and pollution charges paid by all water users. For municipalities and domestic users, these charges are collected by water and sanitation services and then transferred to the Water Agency. These charges correspond to a certain extent to resource costs, defined as the opportunity costs of using water as a scarce resource in time and space. Resource costs equal the difference between the economic value in terms of net benefits of present or future water use (e.g., allocation of emission or water abstraction permits) and the economic value in terms of net benefits of the best alternative water use (now or in the future). Resource costs only arise if alternative water use generates a higher economic value than present or foreseen future water use (i.e., the difference between net benefits is negative). Resource costs are therefore not necessarily confined to water resource depletion (in terms of quantity or quality). They arise because of an inefficient allocation (in economic terms) of water and/or pollution over time and across different water users. Normally, environmental and resource costs are partly recovered through environmental taxes and charges (abstraction and pollution charges).

The highest rates are for water used as drinking water. In addition, the rates are differentiated by source (groundwater or surface water) and by zone, to take into account the relative scarcity of water and the pressure that withdrawal exerts on available water resources. As a result, the rate per m³ of water withdrawn can differ considerably. For example, the rates applied by the Adour-Garonne water agency in 2019-24 range from EUR cent 0.03/m³ for the filling of canals in an area without water deficit to EUR cent 5.8/m³ for potable water abstraction in deficit areas (Table 3.5).

The water abstraction charge reflects the "water pays for water" principle and is generally accepted as fair payment for the use of a scarce resource. However, the rates are too low to have a significant impact on water consumption, making the instrument more of a revenue-raising tool than an economic incentive.

### Table 3.5. Water abstraction rates in the Adour-Garonne basin

| Type of use | Areas with water scarcity | | | Other areas | | |
|---|---|---|---|---|---|---|
| | Rate applied in 2019-24 | | Ceiling set by law | Rate applied in 2019-24 | | Ceiling set by law |
| | Surface water | Groundwater | | Surface water | Groundwater | |
| | EUR cent/m3 | | | EUR cent/m3 | | |
| Gravity irrigation | 1.0 | 1.0 | 1.0 | 0.5 | 0.5 | 0.5 |
| Other irrigation | 1.22 | 0.73 | 7.2 | 0.92 | 0.55 | 3.6 |
| Drinking water | 5.8 | 3.5 | 14.4 | 4.4 | 2.6 | 7.2 |
| Industrial cooling | 0.182 | 0.109 | 1.0 | 0.137 | 0.082 | 0.5 |
| Canal filling | 0.06 | 0.06 | 0.06 | 0.03 | 0.03 | 0.03 |
| Other economic uses | 1.57 | 0.94 | 10.8 | 1.18 | 0.71 | 5.4 |

Source: Notice of deliberation of the Board of Directors of the Adour-Garonne water agency of 19 September 2018.

Another issue is the distribution of the burden between users on the basis of a downstream/upstream and urban/rural "solidarity principle", with households paying much more than agriculture and industry. The related rate differentiation contradicts the polluter pays principle. For example, at the Adour-Garonne water agency, 65% of the revenue from abstraction charges is paid by drinking water companies (and passed on to the water bill), much more than their 11% share of the use of water resources (Table 3.6).

**Table 3.6. Volume abstracted and charging of abstractions in the Adour-Garonne basin**

| Water user sector | Water abstraction | | Charge revenues | |
|---|---|---|---|---|
| | Million m3/year | % | Million EUR/year | % |
| Households | 720 | 11 | 40 | 65 |
| Agriculture | 900 | 14 | 8 | 13 |
| Industrial cooling | 4 700 | 71 | 1 | 2 |
| Hydropower | - | - | 7 | 11 |
| Other economic uses | 320 | 5 | 6 | 10 |
| Total | 6 640 | 100 | 62 | 100 |

Note: - = non-consumptive use.
Source: Adour-Garonne Water Agency (2021[13]), Homepage, https://www.eau-grandsudouest.fr/ (accessed December 2021).

Regardless of the compensation measure in place, conflict due to inter-basin transfers are common. Water transfers are a sensitive strategy to overcome water scarcity needs. Box 3.7 illustrates Korean experience with this challenge. Numerous elements should be reinforced to reduce conflict in the future while ensuring that the water security is achieved across basins and not only at specific locations. Monitoring i) the total water balance across basins to address any asymmetry over time, ii) users consent across regions and iii) economic and non-economic compensation mechanisms matters, in particular during scarcity times.

**Box 3.7. Box inter-regional water transfer dispute in Korea**

Inter-regional water transfer works well if water resources are asymmetrically distributed among senders and receivers and total water availability among them can meet the aggregated water demands at the given compensation level. However, this framework will not be available any longer, if excessive water demand occurs and the compensation level water senders request is beyond what water receivers can afford. This situation has happened when developing countries grow and develop. The inter-regional water dispute between Busan city and its neighbouring provinces in Korea illustrates how increasing water scarcity puts inter-regional water transfer at risk.

Busan Metropolitan City is the second largest city in Korea with 3.5 million people. The city has used Nakdong River as the major source of drinking water. The cities and industries located in the upper stream of Nakdong River - including Gumi - have developed rapidly. However, the quality of Nakdong River has decreased due to influx of improperly treated industrial and household wastewater. The Phenol contamination of Nakdong River from an industrial complex of Gumi City was the decisive incident that made Busan citizens anxious about the safety of their drinking water. Improving water quality of Nakdong River is economically difficult for the Korean government, because many industrial complexes responsible for considerable share of Korean export are located in the upper river basin. It requires important public expenditure to monitor and control all water influx into Nakdong River. Therefore, Busan has tried to diversify its water sources, including through inter-regional water transfer from other regions since 1990s.

In 1996, Korean government made an inter-regional water transfer plan from the downstream of Hwang River in Hapcheon of Gyeongsang Namdo province and Busan city. This plan stimulated fierce opposition of Hapcheon citizens and was cancelled. Due to increasing population and urbanization, Busan faced water quality and scarcity problems at the same time and tried to secure clean water from Nam River dam in Jin-ju city of Gyeongsang Namdo province in 2018. Jin-ju local government and citizens denounced this water transfer plan pointing out increased water scarcity due to additional water intake during dry season and flood risk caused by heightened normal maximum pool level of Nam River dam during rainy season. Busan cancelled its water transfer plan and promised to find alternative ways in 2019.

Lessons learned relevant to Thailand:

- Public consent from the basin of origin over time is a crucial factor to make the water transfer sustainable.
- Economic compensation for water transfer may become ineffective in the long term. Economic value of fresh water will increase due to growing water scarcity along with the economic development of the sending region.

Source: GyeongbukTop, What is the solution to address chronic water allocation dispute among municipalities in Nakdong River Basin in Korea? 2021(https://www.ktn1.net/news/articleView.html?idxno=11984

Source: The Diplomat, The 1962 Johor-Singapore Water Agreement: Lessons Learned. 2021. https://thediplomat.com/2021/09/the-1962-johor-singapore-water-agreement-lessons-learned

Note: Reorganized, edited in English based on the Korean article written in Korean.

### 3.4.2. New water tariff

Thailand has started the process of reviewing its water tariffs for all users, by homogenising the calculation methodology across sectors. Under the new formula, capital operation and maintenance costs should be covered by water users.

Without further information on the new tariff system, no recommendation can be provided in relation to the feasibility of introducing an additional variable to increase revenues for compensation mechanisms. However, taking into account the low water tariff rate, adding an additional cost to the formula may not be the most viable solution in the short them. Currently, water tariffs in Thailand are low. For instance, the charge for raw water is based on a national tariff dating back to the 1940s, while wastewater services are free for most of the population (OECD/ADBI/Mekong Institute, 2020[10]). Adjusting these tariffs is challenging from both a technical and political point of view. However, when comparing peer countries including Indonesia, Vietnam, Philippines, the water tariff level of Thailand is considerably low, as illustrated in Table 3.7. The GDP per capita of Thailand of 2020 was $7,188, nearly twice as much as that of its regional peer countries such as Indonesia ($3,922), Vietnam ($3,525) and the Philippines ($3,323). In other words, Thailand could increase water tariff in exchange of better services.

Low tariffs for water services have two harmful consequences. First, they deprive service providers from the revenues to improve service provision and reach unserved communities. Second, water tariffs are too low to manage water demand (Molle, 2001[14]). While disaggregated data on affordability is lacking, it is worth noting that cheap water usually is a very inefficient way to address affordability issues. This is so as a vast majority of water users could afford to pay more for the service they benefit from. In developed and developing countries, cheap water hurts the poor as it prevents extension of service coverage to unserved communities, who often procure unsafe water from private vendors at a much higher price than public supply.

Table 3.7. Water costs and GDP per capita in some Asian countries

| Country | Cost of water usage (30m3) | National GDP per Capita |
|---|---|---|
| Laos | 0.89 | $2,587 |
| Philippines | 2.37 | $3,323 |
| Vietnam | 3.39 | $3,525 |
| Indonesia | 3.78 | $3,922 |
| Thailand | 1.35 | $7,188 |
| Malaysia | 8.93 | $10,231 |

Note: Based on the table of cost of domestic water use in ADB document and World Bank GDP per capita datasheet as of the 31th December 2020
Source: Water in Asian cities, ADB, 2020 (Andrews, Ynⁱiguez and Asian Development Bank., 2004[15]) and World Bank Data (https://data.worldbank.org/indicator/NY.GDP.PCAP.CD?locations=Z4-8S-Z7)

The new tariff should ensure that there is full cost recovery, across all water sectors. To achieve it, ONWR would require to promote this principle across sectors and Ministries. Several obstacles may limit its implementation in Thailand: 1) policy makers' concern about the strong public opposition to refuse any price increases in public goods especially water and 2) lack of users trust to accept an increase of water tariff in exchange of better services.

ONWR would need to address two main challenges when supporting water tariffs aiming at full cost recovery in the EEC: low willingness to pay of water users and water tariffs impacts on the Consumer Price Index monitored and controlled by the Ministry of Finance. Water is an intermediate good used in countless manufacturing process, increasing water tariff has a direct impact on the Consumer Price Index and indirectly increases food, industrial products and services prices. Therefore, the trade-off between the strong need to increase water tariffs to ensure the sustainability of services and water security and the pressure on keeping it low due to domestic economy requires strong cooperation among the Ministry of Finance and OWNR.

This assumption needs to be checked. First, social expectations vis-à-vis water security and access to water and sanitation services are likely to change as Thailand develops. Second, simple economic analysis would demonstrate that the impact of higher water tariffs on the consumer price index would be minimal.

When affordability issues are documented, they are best addressed through targeted social measures. Setting tariffs at the right level and structuring them appropriately is complicated by the need to address multiple policy objectives (economic, financial, social and environmental). Despite the existence of various water tariff practices around the world, there is no consensus on which tariff structure best balances the objectives of the utility, customers and society as a whole (OECD, 2020[16]).

The efficiency of tariffs as instruments to manage water demand depends on users' response to price signals. The literature suggests that this response is usually limited, in particular in the short term. For example, accompanying measures, such as nudging, can enhance the elasticity of domestic water demand to price (OECD, 2020[16]).

While authorities and service providers allocate considerable amounts of time and efforts to design and adjust tariff structures to accommodate multiple policy objectives, they usually fail to combine efficiency and equity objectives. Increasing-block tariffs - which provide water for basic needs at a lower price - can be socially progressive only when they meet two conditions:

1. highest tariff blocks are set well above the average cost of service provision and income generated serve to cover the costs of the subsidised lower block; and

2. They take into consideration that poor households can actually consume more water than wealthy ones (because they have larger families, or less water-efficient networks or appliances).

In practice well-targeted tariff structures are complicated and difficult to understand: they may be perceived as opaque. They require information on water use and its features (for instance on the size of households, age and physical conditions of individuals, crop production, quality required among others) that are either costly to collect or not accessible to service providers. This explains why sophisticated tariff structures can fail to target the households most in need (OECD, 2020[16]).

Fiscal transfers can be justified to cover part of the cost of water services. Public authorities must pay attention to which fiscal instrument is most appropriate. Different fiscal instruments have distinctive capacities to address the social dimensions of paying for water supply and sanitation services, as well as water for other sectors. The most appropriate fiscal instruments will depend on Thai national context. For example, touristic areas property taxes can be used to capture some of the value added by reliable water supply and sanitation services (OECD, 2020[16]).

Affordability is a multifaceted issue, which does not merely refer to the capacity to foot the water bill. Affordability also relates to how water bills affect users' capacity to meet other essential needs (e.g. food or health care). It relates to the capacity to save (when water bills are issued every quarter or year) and to have stable revenues. It follows that appropriate responses to affordability issues need to combine several dimensions. They can waive or modulate access fees, which can be disproportionate with households' capacities to save or incur debt. They can adjust payment schedules to match users' liquidity or irregular income. They are better delivered through targeted social measures than through the water bill. The most appropriate responses vary according to national and local contexts. They usually combine a capacity to target users most in need of support; low transaction costs, building on existing data and social programmes; and synergies with water conservation measures (OECD, 2020[16]).

## 3.5. Stimulating demand for reuse of treated wastewater in the EEC

In Thailand, the major constraints to wastewater treatment are the high cost of investment and lack of continuous operation and maintenance. This applies to wastewater in the EEC. However, the EEC has started to implement its wastewater plan, focusing on domestic use, including wastewater control and minimization at point sources, public participation, effective law enforcement, and rehabilitation and construction of wastewater treatment facilities.

In relation to industry sector, Chonburi and Rayong provinces have been designated for developing the EEC. In Chonburi province, there is Laem Chabang Industrial Estate, the largest industrial port of Thailand. For Rayong province, there are a lot of industries and Map Ta Phut Industrial Estate is the largest one. To manage industrial wastewater quality, the emphasis is set on the reduction of wastewater at point sources, establishment of a permit system to control industrial discharge, and installation of online monitoring equipment at point sources.

Treated wastewater is a reliable alternative water source in water-scarce regions. Plan for the reuse of treated wastewater plans should be reviewed in consideration of the characteristics and economic situation of the each EEC province. As such, diverse water uses need to be taken into consideration when establishing wastewater reuse plans and strategies: i) agricultural uses such as irrigation of crops, orchards and pastures or aquaculture, ii) industrial uses such as cooling water, process water, aggregate washing, concrete making, soil compaction, dust control, iii) municipal, landscape uses such as irrigation of public parks, recreational and sporting facilities, street cleaning, fire protection systems, toilet flushing, dust control.

Planning for water reuse includes the following considerations:

1. Identify the available quantities of wastewater that could be recycled and how these are placed to address individual needs ;
2. Determine the necessary quality standards or treatment requirements and other requirements ensuring safe use and protection of health and the environment;
3. Identify the different costs (and energy requirements) associated with treatment of the different wastewater sources and with the delivery of treated wastewater to identified users;
4. Determine the funding sources for the development and operation of the reuse schemes and adequate water tariffs. This element can be complemented by who will recover the costs; and
5. Establish systems for control and monitoring to ensure safe use of the treated wastewater for people and the environment and compliance by the operator with legal obligations.

In parallel, the deployment of reclaimed water requires the stimulation of demand for alternative sources of water. This can be achieved by a combination of robust water allocation regimes (putting a cap on freshwater available for abstraction), quality standards for reclaimed water aligned with requirements for targeted uses, and abstraction charges that reflect water scarcity and make reclaimed water competitive and attractive. Different water users have different expectations and reclaimed water becomes a viable option when it comes with guaranteed access to needed volumes at a stable price. This combination allows water users (water utilities, industries and farmers) to factor water availability in their operation and adjust behaviour and use. We turn to this in the following subsections.

Countries such as Israel (see Box 3.8) and Spain which have experienced similar situation in terms of rapid economic growth with limited water resources provide valuable inspirations for Thailand.

---

### Box 3.8. Policies to implement wastewater reuse in Israel

The increasing shortage of freshwater was the major driver for the reform of water allocation arrangements. The average renewable quantity of water dropped to 1.2 million cubic meters per year (MCM/Y) from 1.4 MCM/Y over the last 50 years. At the same time, Israel faced rapid change in demographic (the population multiplied almost twelve-fold over the past 60 years), standard of living (which translate in additional water demand for domestic uses) and economic trends. That combination of increasing scarcity and rising demand put water resources under significant pressure.

The water crisis also resulted from previous policy decisions, which resulted in over-allocated resources. During the first decades of the Israel's existence, water allocation policy gave priority to accelerated economic development, particularly in the agricultural sector, over the naturally available quantities. This caused a continuous and increasing erosion of the operational storage capacity which worsened during drought years, up to a "crisis" when shortage amounted to almost equal the level of annual overall consumption. This has occurred twice since 2000.

Recent water reforms shifted the responsibility for the treatment of water from municipalities to municipal/ regional water companies. The reform aimed to raise efficiency levels and was spurred by concerns about deteriorating water quality, about equity in access to water and economic development. Recent concerns about water shortages or scarcity, climate change and environmental improvement or protection have pushed forward on-going water reforms to increase water re-use and build seawater desalination plants.

---

The reform achieved the following elements for the reuse of treated wastewater for agriculture:

- 87% of wastewater is treated and later re-used, mainly for agriculture. Treated wastewater is also available for industry, gardening, etc.;

- Substituting freshwater with treated wastewater helped to address inter-annual and inter-seasonal variability and built resilient to climate change. For example, during the summer, less freshwater is available and treated wastewater is used to compensate;

- Tariffs vary among treatment facilities. The payment they receive for each cubic meter is significantly higher in summer than winter;

- Entitlements are granted in perpetuity, but conditional upon beneficial use.

As result, 530 million cubic meters of sewage are produced annually in Israel. Israel reuses close to 90% of its wastewater effluent, primarily for irrigation purposes; about 10% goes to environmental uses, including increasing river flows and fire suppression; only 5% percent is discharged into the sea. The flow rate is managed or controlled fully as the water systems are entirely regulated.

Currently, treated wastewater constitutes about 21% of total water consumption in Israel and around 45% of agricultural consumption.

Source: OECD (2015), Water Resources Allocation: Sharing Risks and Opportunities, OECD Studies on Water, OECD Publishing, Paris, https://doi.org/10.1787/9789264229631-en.;

### 3.5.1. Advanced water reuse technologies

A variety of technologies with different nature, processes, and means exists for wastewater treatment. A treatment technology can be employed singly or in combination with other technologies and processes for optimal result. Due to the numerous available technologies and processes, there is a respectively high number of possible flow diagrams for the treatment train that can be adopted, depending on the specific characteristics of each reuse application. The basic principle of wastewater treatment plants is the optimum removal of the various pollutants present in wastewater. The necessary level of wastewater treatment is defined by the effluent limit concentrations, which needs to be fulfilled before the final discharge of the effluent, and by the option of water reuse of this treated effluent. A conventional treatment train usually includes up to two or three treatment stages: primary (preliminary), secondary, and tertiary treatment.

Increasing recognition of treated water as a valuable resource enhances the demand for water reuse, especially in the urban environment. Water reuse for non-potable applications in urban areas can significantly contribute to potable water supplies conservation.

Water reuse applications take place mainly in large centralized treatment facilities. If water reclamation is the target, then advanced treatment technologies should be included in the treatment train. A variety of different technologies could be available to achieve an optimum effluent quality suitable for reuse applications in the EEC.

### 3.5.2. Water Sensitive Urban Design

Water sensitive urban design which includes nature solutions to collect water as part of the water reuse cycle. This supplements treatment of effluents in wastewater treatment plants, by collecting rainwater and making it available for (non-potable) uses in urban environments.

Water Sensitive Urban Design (WSUD) integrates urban water cycle management with urban planning and design, with the aim of mimicking natural systems to minimize negative impacts on the natural water cycle and receiving waterways and bays. It offers an alternative to the traditional conveyance approach to storm water management by acting at the source, thereby reducing the required size of the structural storm water system. It seeks to minimize impervious surfaces, reuse water on site, incorporate retention basins to reduce peak flows, and incorporate treatment systems to remove pollutants. WSUD also provides the opportunity to achieve multiple benefits though sustainable urban water management.

The key principles of WSUD are:

- Protect and enhance natural water systems within urban environments.
- Integrate storm water treatment into the landscape, maximizing the visual and recreational amenity of developments.
- Improve the quality of water draining from urban developments into receiving environments.
- Reduce runoff and peak flows from urban developments by increasing local detention times and minimizing impervious areas.
- Minimize drainage infrastructure costs of development due to reduced runoff and peak flows.

**Figure 3.2. Water sensitive urban design water balance and water management tools**

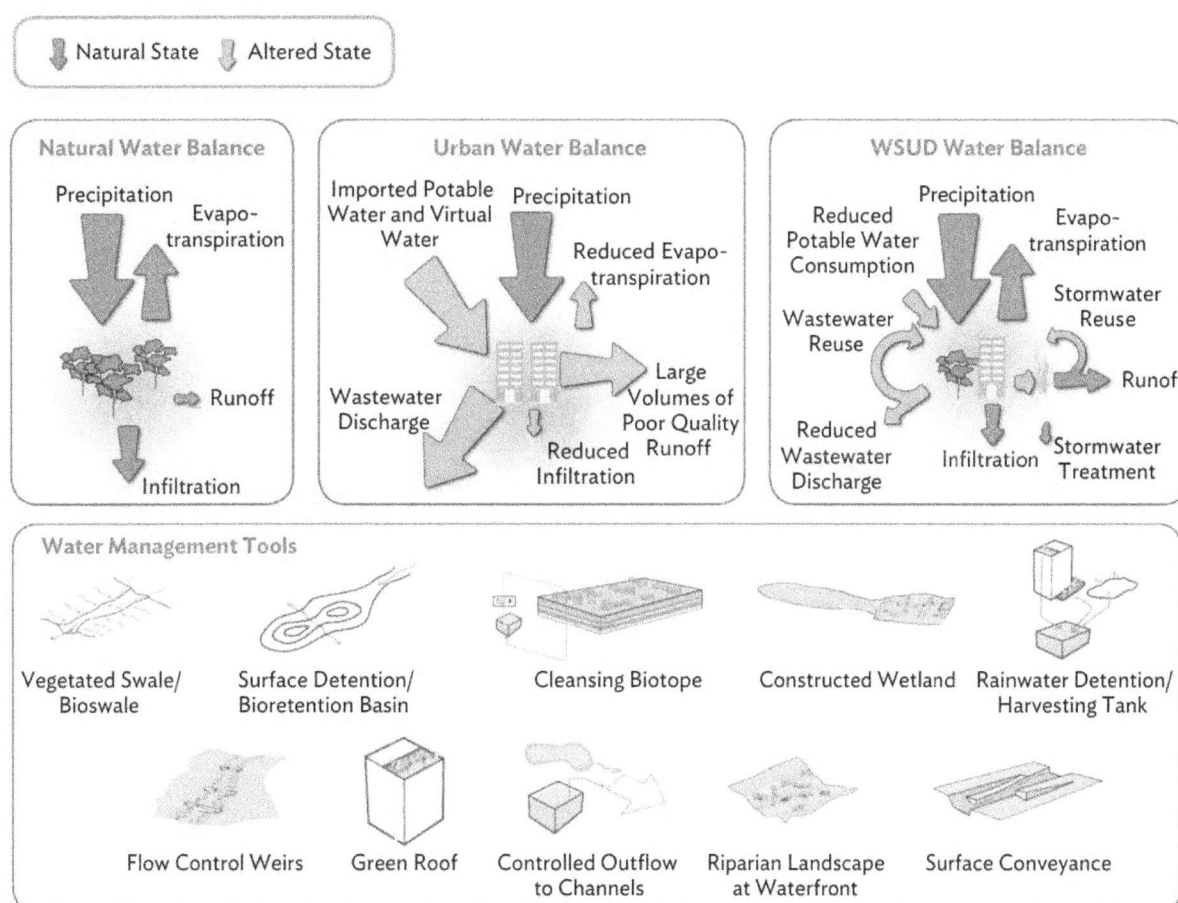

Source: A. Hoban and T.H.F. Wong. WSUD Resilience to Climate Change. Paper presented at the first Australian National Hydropolis Conference. Perth. 8–11 October, 2006

The WSUD concept and tools are flexible enough to be inserted in different types of urban development. Large open space with waterways, a building unit, civic plaza, and hardscapes (car park and roads) are typical options for application. In any case, a soft scape plays a significant role in storing, treating, and conveying water for various purposes: flood mitigation, runoff harvesting and reuse, heat mitigation, and recreational use with added ecological value.

Figure 3.3. WSUD Applications

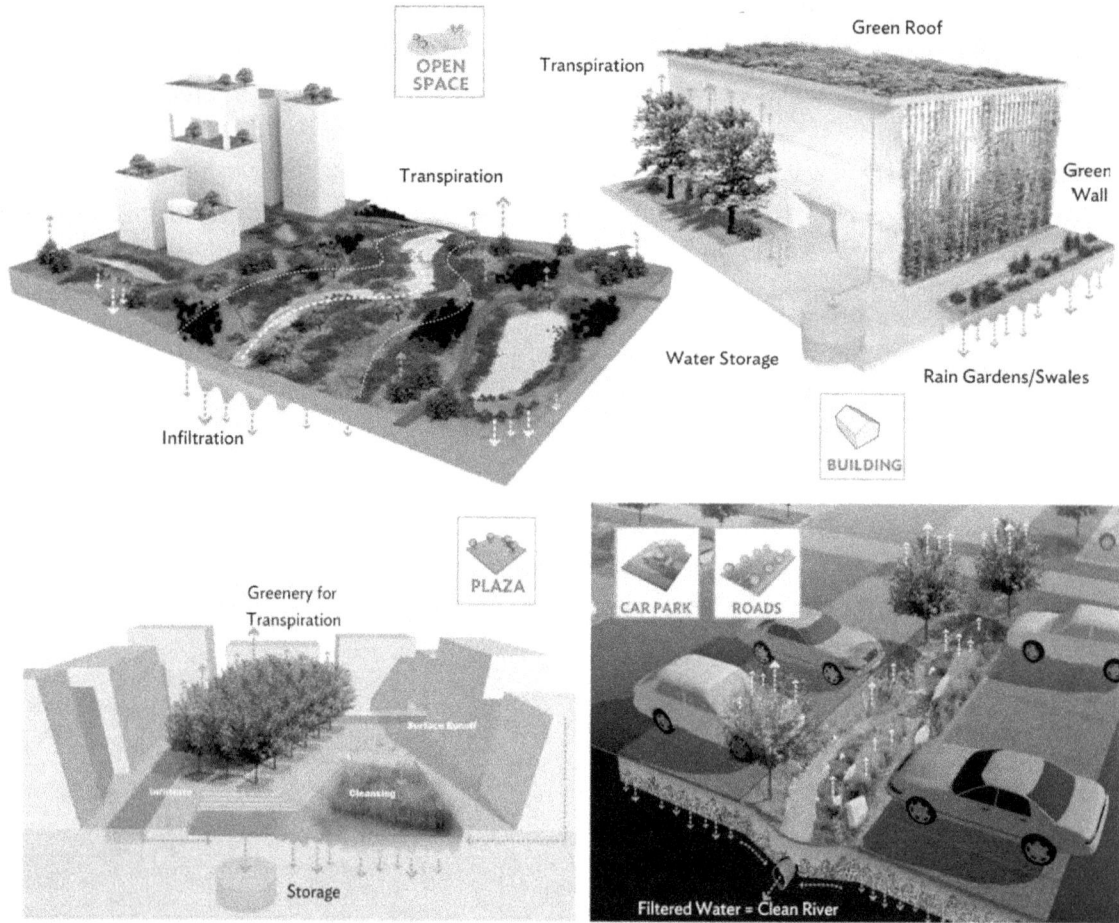

A notable example is the Cheonggyecheon Stream in Seoul, South Korea, a restored 11 km stream in the middle of the city that was once topped by a highway (Figure 3.3. ). The project has shown an improvement in its recreational value by providing publicly accessible equipment for residents and tourists. By using the presence and natural process of water, it has reduced the heat island effect, with the stream acting as a cooling mechanism facilitating thermal comfort while managing storm water runoff.

Figure 3.4. Cheonggyecheon Stream, Seoul, Korea – Restoration of Cheonggyecheon river

Source: Transforming Cities through Water-Sensitive Principles and Practices, Tony H.F. Wong, Briony C. Rogers,Rebekah R. Brown

*Recommendations on increasing users demand*

Acceptability by the social communities or households is a requisite for the deployment of alternative water systems. The main challenge regards potable reuse.

Indirect potable reuse, meaning where reclaimed water is discharged into a water body before being used in the potable water system, has successfully been implemented in Australia, Europe, Singapore and the United States. As noted by Marsden Jacob Associates (2006), "the key issue is not whether the science or the engineering are feasible, but the extent to which indirect potable reuse will be accepted by the public (OECD, 2015[17]).

Direct reuse is more sensitive. Singapore, which produces New Water (Box 3.9) complying with the most stringent requirements for industrial uses, finds it difficult to sell extra-safe water to consumers. Trust in standards, in the processes that prevailed to their definition, and in compliance enforcement contributes to (but does not guarantee) acceptance (OECD, 2015[17]).

Reform of the governance and the institutional framework for water supply and sanitation is a requisite for the public opinion to consider alternative ways of providing water. Changing patterns of water use is a process of long-term institutional transformation. To ensure that water reuse is a viable source of water, policy should focus on facilitating stable predictable arrangements for making policy decisions such as guaranteed volume during scarcity times. This should be done including civic groups to reassure and inform the public. This implies long-term institutions in charge of water re-use for continuous negotiation among diverse stakeholders about conditions, meanings, values and relationships (OECD, 2015[17]).

Based on other countries experiences, key factors can contribute to the acceptability of reuse water. First, scarcity is the main driver to awake the public interest in alternative sources of water. Second, the possibility of providing permanent supply even during scarcity times. And finally when compared with other sources of water, such as desalinisation, energy consumption is lower[1] (Schaum, Lensch and Cornel, 2015[18]). These factors combined with financial incentives can make reuse water a major source of supply in the EEC.

*Water Tariffs*

Water tariff, as indicated by the OECD Council Recommendation on Water, should be based on the principle that tariffs enable full cost recovery including cost of water conveyance, piping systems and wastewater treatment (OECD, 2021[11]).

In the EEC, setting prices right for water could be the first step towards stimulating markets for water reuse. From a revenue side, the financial attractiveness of reuse water systems is limited by the fact that revenues coming from water tariffs and other charges and in most cases, they do not reflect the positive externalities for the society at large. Typically, revenue streams from non-potable reused water are limited because only a few applications qualify, and the willingness to pay for them is low. This is so for two reasons: first, the price of potable water does not reflect its full cost and second, non-potable uses are valued less by the community and the customers than drinking water (OECD, 2015[17]).

This illustrates a market failure which is typical for environmental policy and which can legitimate policy interventions. It follows that alternative water systems can only be deployed when water-related institutions and regulations are transformed into enabling frameworks, a prerequisite for the deployment of reclaimed water (OECD, 2015[17]).

In Thailand, and in particular the EEC, the appropriate pricing strategy for water reuse should be designed and implemented as part of a wider pricing strategy including tariffs for water reuse, conventional water supply and wastewater treatment, as well as other instruments (e.g. water charges). The application of unmodified pricing principles for conventional water supply, based on cost-recovery considerations only, is not always relevant or appropriate for reclaimed water. Whereas the overall objective of pricing strategies for water reuse should always be cost-recovery, pricing strategies must adopt a system-wide approach – which considers: (i) all components of the system, i.e. water reuse as well as conventional water supply and waste water treatment; (ii) all costs included in the system; and (iii) all benefits (also environmental benefits) (ACTeon, 2016[19]). In addition, water tariffs for reclaimed water need to be regulated through their design, approval and enforcement to avoid their fluctuation over time and increase transparency for consumers.

Reclaimed water consumption could increase for the industrial sector, in particular in Rayong province, if the production cost is not higher than freshwater, reclaimed water quality meets the quality requirements and constant volume is ensured even during scarcity times. According to representatives of industrial sector, most manufacturers in EEC have their own water storage facilities to address unexpected water shortage and already use reclaimed water in their production process. The percentage of reuse water used is almost 50 percent. According to the interviews, the main barrier to increase further the use of reuse water is its cost, compared with fresh water. It is therefore essential that freshwater charges and tariffs reflect the cost of the service, including the resource cost (i.e. the opportunity cost of using water when it is scarce).

Water supply affects the production and manufacturing process of most goods and products. Therefore industrial stakeholders are taking water price and stable supply into account to ensure profitability. Industries analyse the cost of their water use and reliability of supply. They will opt for the water resource (freshwater versus reclaimed water) which is the most beneficial and which minimise the risk of production failure due to water shortage.

The total amount of water saved from using reuse water in the industrial sector may be lower than the agriculture sector. However, industrial sector is less sensitive to psychological factor of reuse water, unlike agriculture and households. Currently, farmers can irrigate with fresh bulk water without any cost; therefore, they have no incentive to purchase reclaimed water. Considering the EEC development plan to make this region, the high-tech industrial hub of Thailand, promoting reuse water for the industry would support water security in the region.

In summary, lowering the production cost of reuse water is a key factor to increase its consumption. Reuse water cost can be reduced through: (1) developing in country new development of wastewater treatment technologies through public and private research and development, (2) importing advanced wastewater treatment technology from world class reclaimed water facility operators (Fu, Pietrobelli and Soete, 2010[20]), (3) reaching economy of scale by grouping individual wastewater facilities and (4) designing economic incentive for those who increase their usage of reuse water including tax exemption or reductions.

### 3.5.3. Guaranteed volume

Water reuse can be particularly attractive in the EEC due to drought risks, because it can allow permanent supply even during scarcity time. For industry production, which may require a constant volume even during drought periods, permanent supply can be a decisive factor for its settlement in a region such as the EEC. In addition, reuse water, by unlocking an additional water supply source for some sectors such as industry, could reduce competition between users of freshwater. For large agriculture producers, having high value crops requiring precise irrigation, reclaimed water can be an appropriate option instead of lacking supply and losing the production. In addition, freshwater users may be less subject to water restrictions in periods of water scarcity.

### 3.5.4. Water quality standards for different users

In the EEC, treatment of alternative sources of water adjusted to the quality standards of different applications can increase its demand. There are two broad categories of applications: potable and non-potable ones. Non potable uses include irrigation (for some type of crops, parks and golf courses), most industrial applications, some uses for households, including outdoor uses (such as gardening) and indoor applications (e.g. flushing toilets or washing machines). Alternative sources of water can be used for direct or indirect potable reuse (water is discharged into a water body before being used in the potable water system) (OECD, 2015[17]).

Water sector regulators need to be prepared to monitor water quality from a variety of different sources in multiple settings (in central plants, commercial and industrial buildings, and private houses). This requires capacity, financial and human resources.

As the EEC continues with its economic development, stringent standards for wastewater treatment and discharge will be required to stimulate supply and demand for reclaimed water. For example, in the European Union, the widespread of tertiary treatment, due to the introduction of Directives increasing environmental standards, contributed to wastewater reuse expansion (European Commission, 2019[21]). As part of the overall perception of sewage as an important source of water, and if treated wastewater is to be used for agricultural irrigation, sewage treatment must be done according to strict standards so that the effluent quality is safe for irrigation of all agricultural crops and for discharge in to water sources (rivers and aquifers).

### 3.5.5. Communication

It is key to raise awareness among citizens and policy makers that current levels of water security are jeopardised by climate change, urbanisation, and demographic and economic trends. This is a requisite to trigger policy and behavioural change.

Some countries has overcome this challenge through targeted communication campaigns. In Australia, research has shown how public perceptions of alternative sources of water (including reclaimed water) have changed over the last 10 years. Initial concerns for public health hazard now leave way to less resistance to use reclaimed water for garden watering and cleaning uses. This was achieved through targeting opinion leader groups and the media (OECD, 2015[17]).

If Thailand wants to scale up reclaimed water and unlock its potential as additional source of water, communication would need to be a main pillar of its strategy. Numerous cities such as Singapore have developed communication strategies specific to reclaimed water, to raise awareness among the population by highlighting its safety and numerous advantages in particular in regions already suffering water insecurity; see Box 3.9.

---

**Box 3.9. NEWater communication strategy for reuse water**

Singapore has developed one of the world's most advanced water reuse programmes. The reuse programme, called NEWater, relies on advanced microfiltration, reverse osmosis and ultraviolet exposure to clean and treat wastewater for potable consumption. NEWater has been recognised as an international model for innovation in water management, most recently winning the Environmental Contribution of the Year award from the London-based group Global Water Intelligence.

In 2003, the Public Utilities Board (PUB), Singapore's national water agency, introduced NEWater as one of Singapore's Four National Taps (which also include local catchment water, imported water and desalinated water). It is high-grade reclaimed water produced from treated used water that has undergone stringent purification and treatment process using advanced dual membrane (microfiltration and reverse osmosis) and ultraviolet technologies. It has passed over 130 000 scientific tests and exceeds the drinking water standards set by the World Health Organization and the US Environmental Protection Agency. NEWater is used primarily for non-potable industrial purposes at wafer fabrication parks, industrial estates and commercial buildings. During dry months, NEWater is used to top up the reservoirs and blended with raw water before undergoing treatment at the waterworks before being supplied for the drinking water supply.

Prior to the development of NEWater, Singapore had to rely heavily on local catchments and imported water from Johor in Malaysia as its key water sources. However, these two traditional sources are weather-dependent. While reclaiming used water is not a new concept, what is significant for Singapore is the wide-scale implementation and widespread public acceptance of NEWater for indirect potable use. This is part of an overall strategy to raise awareness of the population, stressing a new approach to water management by communicating to the public the need to look at water as a renewable resource that could be used over and over again. The price of NEWater is cheaper than that of potable water and this has encouraged many industries to switch to NEWater. Strict enforcement of used water discharge also plays an important role in ensuring that water reclamation plants are able to function as designed, which then supply part of the treated effluent to the NEWater plants. Water reclamation technology is relevant to other water-scarce regions. From an energy perspective, it is about one quarter of what desalination would require. It is from this perspective that NEWater holds tremendous promise for developing cities.

Source: OECD (2016), Water Governance in Cities, OECD Studies on Water, OECD Publishing, Paris, https://doi.org/10.1787/9789264251090-en.

# References

ACTeon (2016), *Cost, pricing and financing of water reuse against natural water re-sources*, https://doi.org/10.13140/RG.2.2.12270.41289 (accessed on 2022). [19]

Adour-Garonne Water Agency (2021), *Homepage*, https://www.eau-grandsudouest.fr/ (accessed on 10 December 2021). [13]

ANA (2016), "Plano de recursos hídricos da bacia hidrográfica do rio Piancó-Piranhas-Açu - Resumo executivo", Agência Nacional de Águas, http://piranhasacu.ana.gov.br/produtos/PRH_PiancoPiranhasAcu_ResumoExecutivo_300620 16.pdf. [8]

Andrews, C., C. Yñiguez and Asian Development Bank. (2004), *Water in Asian cities : utilities' performance and civil society views*, Asian Development Bank. [15]

da Silva Santos, A. (2021), "Ex-post evaluation of the socio-economic consequences of the Integration Project of the São Francisco River with Watersheds of the Northern Northeast", *CADERNOS DE FINANÇAS PÚBLICAS*, Vol. 21/1, https://publicacoes.tesouro.gov.br/index.php/cadernos/article/view/128 (accessed on 4 January 2022). [9]

de Sousa Freitas, M. (2021), "The Piancó-Piranhas-Açu Hydrographic Basin Face to the 2012-2020 Drought Event", *Brazilian Journal of Animal and Environmental Research*, Vol. 4/1, pp. 1033-1046, https://doi.org/10.34188/bjaerv4n1-084. [7]

EEC Office (2019), "EEC Brochure 2019 (EN)". [1]

European Commission (2019), *Evaluation of the Council Directive 91/271/EEC of 21 May 1991, concerning urban waste-water*, https://ec.europa.eu/environment/water/water-urbanwaste/pdf/UWWTD%20Evaluation%20SWD%20448-701%20web.pdf (accessed on 2022). [21]

European Environmental Agency (2017), *Water management in Europe: price and non-price approaches to water conservation*, https://www.eea.europa.eu/publications/water-management-in-europe-price. [6]

Fu, X., C. Pietrobelli and L. Soete (2010), *The Role of Foreign Technology and Indigenous Innovation in Emerging Economies: Technological Change and Catching Up*, http://www.iadb.org. [20]

Molle, F. (2001), *Water pricing in Thailand : theory and practice*. [14]

OECD (2022), *Fostering Water Resilience in Brazil: Turning Strategy into Action*, OECD Studies on Water, OECD Publishing, Paris, https://doi.org/10.1787/85a99a7c-en. [12]

OECD (2021), *Toolkit for Water Policies and Governance: Converging Towards the OECD Council Recommendation on Water*, OECD Publishing, Paris, https://doi.org/10.1787/ed1a7936-en. [11]

OECD (2020), *Addressing the social consequences of tariffs for water supply and sanitation.*, https://www.oecd.org/officialdocuments/publicdisplaydocumentpdf/?cote=ENV/WKP(2020)13 &docLanguage=En (accessed on 2022). [16]

OECD (2016), *Mitigating Droughts and Floods in Agriculture: Policy Lessons and Approaches*, OECD Studies on Water, OECD Publishing, Paris, https://doi.org/10.1787/9789264246744-en. [3]

OECD (2015), *Alternative Ways of Providing water. Emerging options and their policy implications*, OECD, https://www.oecd.org/env/resources/42349741.pdf. [17]

OECD (2015), *Water Resources Allocation: Sharing Risks and Opportunities*, OECD Studies on Water, OECD Publishing, Paris, https://doi.org/10.1787/9789264229631-en. [2]

OECD (2015), *Water Resources Governance in Brazil*, OECD Studies on Water, OECD Publishing, Paris, https://doi.org/10.1787/9789264238121-en. [5]

OECD/ADBI/Mekong Institute (2020), *Innovation for Water Infrastructure Development in the Mekong Region*, The Development Dimension, OECD Publishing, Paris, https://doi.org/10.1787/167498ea-en. [10]

ONWR (2019), *The management of water resources*, https://pubhtml5.com/gvhf/rvua/basic. [4]

Schaum, C., D. Lensch and P. Cornel (2015), "Water reuse and reclamation: a contribution to energy efficiency in the water cycle", *Journal of Water Reuse and Desalination*, Vol. 5/2, pp. 83-94, https://doi.org/10.2166/wrd.2014.159. [18]

## Notes

[1] The energy consumption for non-potable reuse is only about one-quarter of that for desalination. Economic evaluations show identical trends for annual costs (Schaum, Lensch and Cornel, 2015[18])

# 4 Financing water supply and sanitation

To achieve its ambitious policy objectives, Thailand would benefit from strengthening its capacity to finance water supply and sanitation (both capital expenditure and operation and maintenance costs). The chapter explores several avenues: economic regulation for water supply and sanitation services; benchmarking the performance of water utilities; and blended finance. A range of smart water technologies are presented as well, which can add value for money.

Thailand has made impressive progress to reach some indicators of the Sustainable Development Goal (SDG) 6 in the last decades. In 2020, the country had 100% of the population using an improved drinking water source and sanitation facility. However, in 2020, only 26% of the population was using safely managed sanitation services and only 24% of the wastewater flow was safely treated, being one of the lowest in the region with Lao People's Democratic Republic and Mongolia (UN Water, 2022[1]).

The main drivers for future investment needs in water supply and sanitation include population growth and urbanisation, economic growth (and raising social expectations) and the need to adapt to a changing climate. These drivers trigger additional investment needs to adjust to shifting circumstances. It is not clear how these drivers are reflected in Thai plans to extend coverage and improve quality of service, in both urban and rural settings.

Moreover, the information shared does not seem to reflect financial needs for the operation, maintenance and renewal of existing and future water and sanitation services. These costs tend to be more challenging than funding the capital investment to build infrastructures. Failing to do so can deprive service operators from the revenues they need[1], accelerate the decay of existing infrastructure and enhance the need to rebuild facilities sooner than expected. Recent upsurge in energy prices confirms that operational efficiency is critical for a sustainable water sector. Financing operational efficiency and adequate maintenance requires a robust and sustainable business model that contributes to several policy objectives, including inclusive access to service and rural livelihood, now and in the future.

In parallel to its SDG goals, Thai government continues its strategy to attract private investments, focusing in industry and tourism sectors. This is illustrated by the Asian Development Bank 2021-2025 strategy programmes and projects in Thailand, focused on *"helping Thailand achieve prosperity and sustainability through private sector-led growth and knowledge solutions"*. Financing for private sector operations will target environmental solutions: sustainable energy, transport and agricultural development (Asian Development Bank, 2022[2]). Although the private sector is extremely active in Thailand (World Bank, 2022[3]), the water and sanitation sector has not yet been able to attract private and commercial finance.

To increase the volume of finance available for water supply and sanitation services in Thailand, a number of requisites need to be in place. The first is operational efficiency of existing services. This is a condition to efficient allocation of (public and private) funding, willingness to pay of domestic water users, and minimising financing needs in the future (avoiding rapid decay of existing assets). Then, it becomes feasible to consider accessing a range of private and commercial sources of finance. Here, private and commercial finance does not refer to the private operation of water services[2]. It refers to access to bank loans or capital markets to finance investment and heavy maintenance.

This section focuses on tools that can enhance the performance of water supply and sanitation services, as a condition to make the best use of available assets and available sources of finance and a requisite to attract additional sources of finance from the private sector. Three tools are particularly adjusted to the Thai context:

- Economic regulation for water supply and sanitation services. Economic regulation has a pivotal role to play to support the design of a tariff policy for water supply and sanitation services, to benchmark the performance of water service providers (with a view to enhance performance), to build trust in the sector (and attract the attention of domestic commercial finance).
- Benchmarking the performance of water utilities (criteria to assess, monitor and compare performance; incentives to align with the best performers). This can lead to discussions on the appropriate size of service providers (to reap economies of scale and scope) and incentives to transition towards a sustainable and cost-effective sector[3].
- Smart water technologies. They can facilitate data collection and processing in view to monitor technical efficiency of networks and assets. They can also contribute to better information of users.

The last section focuses on blended finance as a way to use available development and public finance to crowd in private and commercial sources of finance. As mentioned above, blended finance is not a panacea and only delivers if the sector is properly regulated; hence the relevance of the following discussion on economic regulation, operational performance and smart water technologies.

## 4.1. Economic regulation

Currently, several authorities are in charge of regulating water and sanitation service provision in Thailand. Regulatory responsibilities are divided across several bodies such as the Ministry of Interior, ONWR, National Water Resources Commission, Prime Minister Office, Ministry of Industry, Ministry of Agriculture and Cooperatives, Bureau of budget and Ministry of Natural Resources and Environment. The Ministry of Health monitors compliance with national standards, by regularly testing water samples from rural and urban areas. However, limited resources restrict its implementation such as funding constraints, inadequate numbers of skilled graduates and recruitment practices (WHO, 2015[4]).

This section considers the benefit and the options to enhance economic regulation, as a tool that can enhance the performance of water and sanitation services operators and thereby increase their creditworthiness and the financial sustainability of the sector. Economic regulation comes in addition to the definition of performance standards set by health and environmental authorities. It is a requisite for robust performance monitoring and enhancement (see next section).

As indicated in the Recommendation of the OECD Council on water, countries should "ensure that sound water management regulatory frameworks are effectively implemented and enforced in pursuit of the public interest" (OECD, 2021[5]).

Comprehensive, coherent and predictable regulatory frameworks founded on effective regulatory policies and institutions are essential for setting the rules, standards and guidelines to achieve water policy outcomes. Sound regulation serves to ensure that services function efficiently while meeting important social and environmental goals. It also builds public trust in the administration as an effective rule maker (OECD, 2021[5]).

Different types of regulatory frameworks exist to discharge regulatory functions in relation to water services. Aside from self-regulation, major regulatory models include: regulation by government; regulation by contract, which specifies the regulatory regimes in legal instruments (the French model); independent regulation (Anglo-American model); and the outsourcing of regulatory functions to third parties, which makes use of external contractors to perform activities such as tariff reviews, benchmarking and dispute resolution (OECD, 2021[5]).

The third model, the establishment of dedicated regulatory bodies for water and sanitation services is the most common response to some of the challenges of regulatory frameworks for water services. It has also accompanied the reform of the water industry that many countries have undergone over the past two decades, in particular in the trend towards corporatisation[4] of water operators and the consolidation of water service provision. While independent from local and national authorities, economic regulation for water and sanitation services can be bundled together with (or discharged by) a regulator covering other sectors (such as energy supply, for instance).

Economic regulators for water and sanitation services interact with a broad range of institutions, at national or subnational level. This framework typically involves line ministries (environment or natural resources) in charge of water policies, health department in charge of water quality standards and ministries of environment in charge of effluents. Various public agencies, e.g. environmental protection agencies, also play a role in specific issues of water regulation (OECD, 2015[6]).

**Thailand authorities would benefit from designating a single entity in charge of the economic regulation of the water and sanitation sector**. Based on other countries experience, the key features of robust economic regulation for the sector are: (1) the regulator can independently oversee the sector and (2) has the required resources to fulfil its role and impose sanctions.

Several arguments justify providing regulatory powers to an entity for the water and sanitation sector in Thailand:

1. The water and sanitation services sector is a typical example of a monopolist sector. Water companies constitute natural monopolies since the costs of production are lesser in the case of a single producer. Consequently, the water and sanitation services market is characterised by a low level of competition and important restrictions on the entrance of new players. Regulation is justified on the ground that it ought to prevent market power issues arising from a natural monopoly and to protect customers. In the absence of regulation, water operators can be tempted to neglect the quality or the cost-efficiency of services (OECD, 2015[6]).

2. The sector also displays important asymmetry of information. The water operators own information which the responsible public authorities and the consumers do not have access to (e.g. on the state of the asset, maintenance needs, or the cost of service provision). This asymmetry of information may lead to market abuse by the monopolist operators and cause mistrust amongst consumers with regard to the quality or costs of services provided. A transparent access to water and sanitation services data can reduce the risks of information asymmetry (OECD, 2015[6]).

3. The water sector needs to balance a range of economic, social and environmental interests. Water is essential for the lives, health and social protection of citizens. Therefore, water services must fulfil a number of requirements such as universality, continuity, quality of service, equality of access, affordability and transparency. At the same time, the provision of water and sanitation services has a cost – important investments and management and operating costs are involved – that needs to be covered in the most efficient way to ensure its sustainability over time. In the absence of competition and considering information asymmetry, the management of trade-offs across various interests requires public intervention (OECD, 2015[6]).

4. The water sector generates important externalities, in particular in relation to public health, the economy and the environment. The quality of water has strong impacts on public health, which justify the involvement of the ministry of health to define and set the quality standards for drinking water and wastewater treatment. The way wastewater is treated can also impact the environment, and, if ignored or badly managed, generate pollution and negatively impact water availability, environmental services and productive activities (farming, fishing and tourism) downstream (OECD, 2015[6]). Again, as market mechanisms fail to consider these externalities, economic regulation is required to ensure cost-effective service provision.

Thai authorities could benefit from setting a single body in charge of economic regulation of water and sanitation services, tasked with the regulatory functions presented in Table 4.1.

### Table 4.1. Typology of economic regulatory functions for water and sanitation services

| Regulatory functions | Definition |
|---|---|
| Tariff regulation | Establishing a tariff methodology and/or setting and updating prices or supervising the tariff setting process, determining tariffs by consumer group, establishing caps on revenues or rate of return on investment |
| Defining public service obligations/social regulation | Setting public service obligations (including requirements on access to services) and performance requirements for operators. |
| Defining technical/industry and service standards | Developing the standards that underpin the technical modalities and level of service delivery. |
| Setting incentives for efficient use of water resources | Establishing incentives or specific schemes to promote efficient water resource use. |
| Setting incentives for efficient investment | Establishing incentives or specific schemes to promote efficient investment. |
| Promoting innovative technologies | Establishing incentives or specific schemes to promote innovative technologies. |
| Promoting demand management | Establishing incentives or specific schemes to promote reduced water demand. |
| Analysing water utilities' investment plans/business plans | In some cases, the regulator may be asked to approve the business plan or the investment plan of utilities |
| Information and data gathering | Collecting data from operators and undertaking market research to identify trends and potential risks |
| Monitoring of service delivery performance | Monitoring of the performance of water services against a set of targets or of performance indicators. This can involve the benchmarking of water utilities. |
| Licensing of water operators | Granting or approving licences for the operation of water systems. |
| Supervision of contracts with (public or private) operators | The obligations granted by public authorities to a specific utility may be detailed in a specific contract (it is usually the case when a private actor is brought in). The regulator may be tasked with the supervision of the contract. |
| Supervising utilities' financing activities | Monitoring the financial schemes of water utilities (e.g. bond issuance, equity investments). |
| Carrying management audits on utilities | Auditing and/or approving the business plans of utilities. |
| Customer engagement | Consulting with customers on regulatory issues; communicating regulatory decisions to the public. |
| Consumer protection and dispute resolution | Handling consumer complaints about regulated entities. |
| Advice and advocacy | Providing advice for policy making and project implementation; identifying opportunities for reforms; encouraging improvements to the regulatory framework. |

Source: OECD (2015), *The Governance of Water Regulators*, OECD Studies on Water, OECD Publishing, Paris, https://doi.org/10.1787/9789264231092-en.

As mentioned above, these functions can be bundled with similar functions related to energy supply or other services. Economic regulation of water services can be discharged by a sector-specific regulator, a multi-sector regulator, a competition authority or similar agencies. Critical factors here are expertise in economic analyses to set appropriate levels of ambition in terms of operational efficiency and cost-effectiveness; to review investment plans and financing strategies; to review operational performance, to set incentives, rewards and sanctions based on actual performance; to engage with service providers and users.

## 4.2. Benchmarking the performance of water and sanitation utilities

According to the Department of Water Resources and Department of Local Administration, four sets of criteria are used to evaluate the performance of water providers including water quality, water quantity, pressure on pipeline and operation efficiency of facilities. However, none of the departments use the performance results as criteria for economic incentive. The Department of Local Administration hosts a contest to choose the best water service provider of the year. According to the interviews, however, no financial and other regulatory benefit are provided to the winner, other than public recognition. This section explores how benchmarking can be arranged and combined with economic incentives to enhance the performance of WSSS operators.

### 4.2.1. Performance indicators

Performance indicators allow the contracting authority to measure the performance of the operator in a more objective and transparent way. Indicators need to cover the multiple dimensions of service provision, in relation to health, environment, equity (including universal access and affordability) and cost-efficiency (a condition to other dimensions). Environmental and health authorities set performance targets in their domain and need to be closely involved in the definition of performance criteria.

Incentives need to be in place to rewards performance and sanction failure to achieve targets. Incentives can take many forms. Some are financial, such as easy access to (public) finance for well performing operators, or penalties for those who fail to perform. Some are non-financial, such as lax supervision of well-performing operators and more stringent control for others. Where operators are corporatized and engage in contractual arrangements with (local or national) authorities, performance-based contracts can provide the appropriate incentives: the bonus and penalty system built into performance-based contracts should be directly linked to the achievement of the performance indicators (see next section).

Based on other countries experience (OECD, 2011[7]), Thailand could benefit from setting performance indicators taking into account the following good practices:

- Indicators should be few and easy to monitor and verify. They should be targeted at the needs of the individual utility and should reflect the most urgent and critical issues to be solved by the operator. A dozen indicators usually cover the main dimensions of performance. Large number of indicators can be counterproductive, in particular at the beginning of the process.

- Investment indicators alone may not be effective as they do not necessarily translate into actual service improvements.

- Providing a clear definition of the indicators is crucial. Indicators need to be defined in terms of levels, timeframe for their achievement and methodologies for their monitoring, calculation, measuring and revision. Having these methodologies agreed upon well in advance between parties is key in order to avoid future conflict situations.

- Where initial data is limited, it is better to set indicators as increments, or improvements defined in terms of percentage above a baseline, rather than as absolute values. This makes it easier to reflect modifications to the baseline calculations, when necessary.

- Technical auditors can make the system credible and help operators understand the challenges they face and options to address them. However, the powers and responsibilities of the auditor should be carefully defined and balanced with regard to the responsibilities of the operator and the contracting authority.

### 4.2.2. Performance-based contracting arrangements

Performance contracts have emerged as a tool to improve public sector accountability and performance in many countries. Such interest in performance-based contracts is based on governments' increasing focus on bottom-line results and a general shift toward more decentralized management (OECD, 2011[7]).

Performance-based contracting arrangements are intended to promote savings, efficiency, and responsiveness that are expressed in terms of performance expectations linked to budgets, service, and management (OECD, 2011[7]).

These contracts spell out clearly overall targets to be achieved by the contractor but the specific manner employed to achieve such results is left to the contractor's discretion. Thus, results-oriented contracts differ from contracts that focus principally on inputs, means and procedures. The contracts also contain a mutually agreed set of monitored performance targets with financial incentives and penalties. As the contractor's remuneration is tied to its ability to meet set targets, such agreements provide an incentive for the contractor to improve its performance and efficiency (OECD, 2011[7]).

In the case of Thailand, performance-based contracts could be set for public service providers such as Metropolitan Waterworks Authority and Provincial Waterworks Authority and other public or private operators. Setting this type of contract requires a regulator capable to monitor utilities independently and potentially enforce sanctions. Agreements between public sector entities are generally "quasi-contractual" agreements and are not legally enforceable. To be effective and efficient, the use of performance contracting for legally enforceable contracts between public entities, there need to be separate legal entities to ensure independence.

In order to improve the vicious cycle of "low tariffs, low efficiency and high costs, inadequate resources, low service quality, and loss of community support" faced in rural areas in Thailand, Provincial Waterworks Authority could benefit from having contractual relationship. In addition, the involvement of the private sector through Private Public Partnership or the private sector in the EEC could also provide an opportunity to increase formal contracting arrangements in the water sector. The country has some experience on performance based contracts, such as those implemented by Metropolitan Water Works Authority back in 2000 with the World Bank, lessons learned could add to the development of similar contracts by the Provincial Waterworks Authority (World Bank, 2000[8]).

Table 4.2 presents some of the good practices that Thailand authorities could consider when putting in place the legal and regulatory framework for this type of arrangements. These criteria are relevant regardless of the type contract (service contract, management contract, lease, concession, build operate transfer, divestiture).

### Table 4.2. Contractual Agreement criteria good practices

| Criteria | Examples of good practices |
|---|---|
| Duration | The contract provide terms and procedures for extension of the duration. |
| Monitoring | Municipalities or the relevant service authority do fully exercise their responsibility to control and assess the quality of utilities' operation and maintenance |
| Autonomy/competition | Municipality or the relevant service authority are the not sole founder of the operator and thus the operator has autonomy. There is competition in operator selection process. |
| Property ownership/assets | Contracts do provide description of the properties transferred from the municipalities or the relevant service authority to operators. The required state registration and assessment of the transferred property have been completed properly. Contracts do clearly provide operators' rights and limits of use and repair of the property |
| Financial penalties | Contracts provide descriptions on the rights and obligations of the parties in terms of non-compliance. |
| Financing/investment | Contracts do have investment plans and financing plans for the operation and maintenance costs. |
| Remuneration incentives | Operators' remuneration is tied to their performance |
| Performance targets | Contracts do describe time-bound performance targets to be achieved by the operators. |
| Insurance obligation | Contracts do contain insurance provisions. |
| Service operation | Contracts do provide technical parameters of service provision. |
| Guarantees and sanctions | Contracts do specify issues on guarantees, arbitration, financial penalties, and emergency measures. |
| End of contract | Contracts do specify service continuity, assets transfer, and investment settlement at the end of contract |

Source: Guidelines for performance-based contracts between water utilities and municipalities, OECD, 2011. https://www.oecd.org/env/outreach/48656736.pdf

Several mechanisms can be set in place within contractual arrangements to manage conflict resolution. These include given priority to court decision as first instance, and other contracts give preference to amicable non-binding solutions and arbitration. Regardless of the mechanism, the procedures for applying the mechanisms should be well established in the contracts. Arbitration through (a panel of) experts has proven its effectiveness as a working mechanism and is worth considering. However, its application also requires clear rules and procedures. It is important to note that solving conflicts through courts usually costs a lot of time and money and should be a solution of the last resort. Envisaging going to international courts when conflicts arise between parties is a common practice in complex contracts particularly where international operators are involved (OECD, 2011[7]).

Contract monitoring and reporting obligations should be a major element in all performance-based contracts for the water and sanitation services in Thailand. Regular, timely and consistent reporting by the operator on progress with contract implementation allows detecting problems early in the process (OECD, 2011[7]).

Reporting and disclosure of information should be regular but balanced. Too much or too little of it may impose additional and unnecessary burden on both the operator and the contracting authority. Reporting requirements (type of data and information to be collected and monitored, the format in which these will be provided, frequency of submission of reports, procedure for providing feedback by the contracting authority) should be specified in the contract as precisely as possible. If this is not feasible, the contract should envisage a procedure for developing such reporting requirements by some precise date after the contract starts (OECD, 2011[7]).

Given the significant risks involved in water sector contracts, international experience shows that there is a need for explicit mechanisms to ensure contract enforcement and these mechanisms will need to be aligned with the legislation in force in Thailand.

## 4.3. The added value of smart water technologies[5]

### 4.3.1. Smart water management - defined

Technical innovations in information and communications technology (ICT) can be beneficial to the water sector. Smart water management (SWM) is defined as the combination of ICT and water technologies to support water resources management and the delivery of water services. It is designed to tackle increased uncertainties and risks of water-related disasters by developing systematic and effective response mechanisms in a sustainable manner. It does so by making the best use of information and communication technology (ICT) to produce and use large volumes of data in real time to support (and integrate as much as possible) water resources management at different scales, from dam management and flood prevention to detection of leakages and promotion of water use efficiency in homes.

SWM can support progress toward financial sustainability of water and sanitation sector. One way to increase revenues while keeping prices low is to minimise non-revenue water (leakage) and to increase consumption (in particular for drinking purposes). SWM can help detect leakage and inform (domestic) water users about water use and water quality.

Smart water supply systems support safe drinking water with scientific water quantity and quality management and information supply, which is achieved through incorporating ICT into the entire water supply process, from water intake source to faucet. The full spectrum of technology options is sketched below along the water cycle.

## Figure 4.1. Smart management of the water cycle

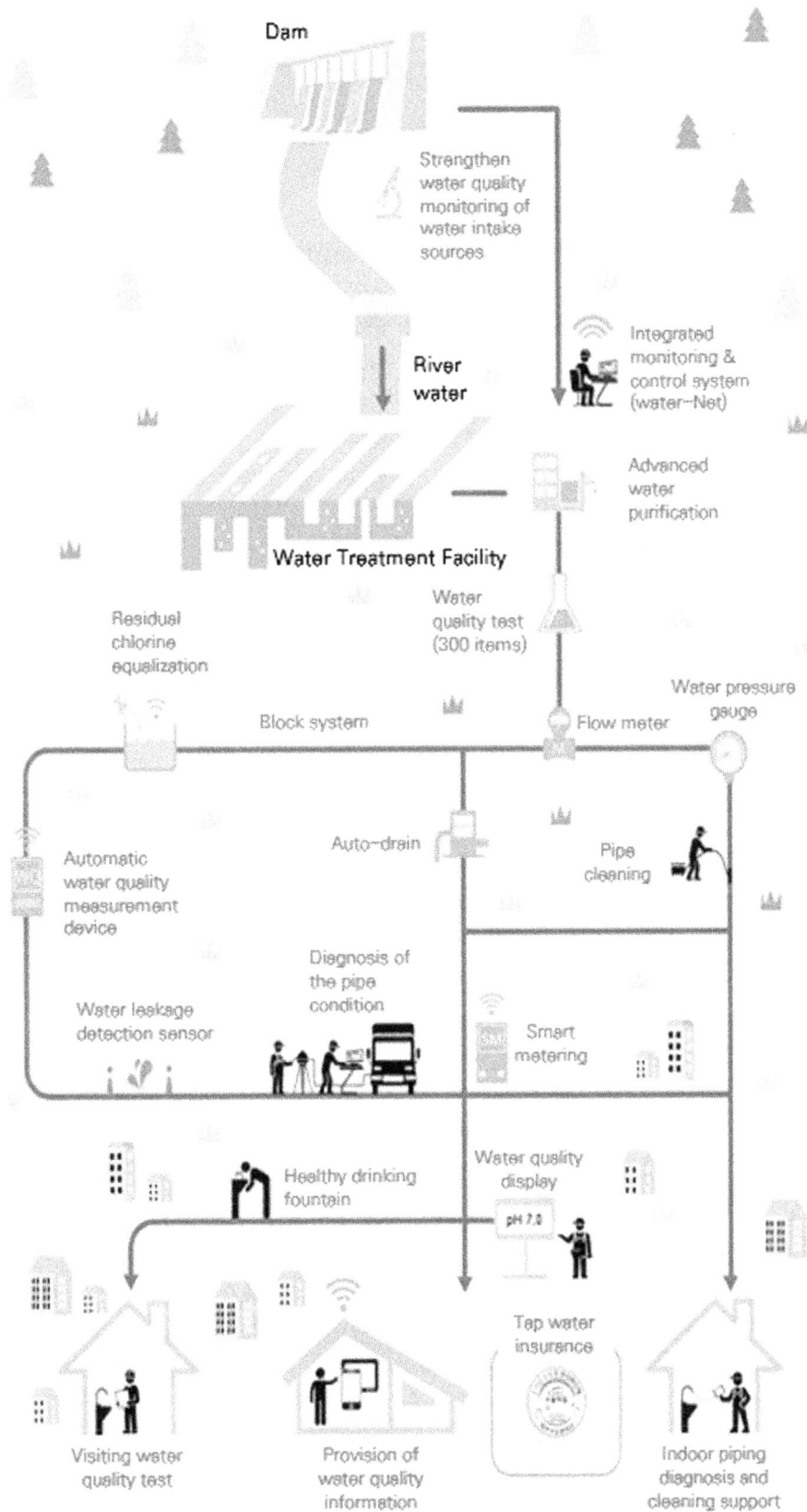

The benefits for water supply and sanitation – from an operator and a user perspective – are captured below.

- Secure and produce safe tap water
  - o Water quality monitoring technology for water intake source (biomonitoring, algae forecasting system, etc.)
  - o Infrastructure for securing water quantity such as diversification of water intake sources
  - o Water treatment technology such as advanced water treatment
- Thoroughly manage tap water supply process
  - o Integrated monitoring and control system for the entire supply process of tap water
  - o Real-time water quantity/quality management technologies for water supply process (block system, smart metering, leak detection system, pipe damage prevention system, re-chlorination, automatic draining, pipe cleaning, automatic water quality meter, etc.)
  - o Pipe network diagnosis technology (exploration and diagnosis of pipe hot tapping)
- Provision of consumer-oriented tap water service
  - o Real-time water quality information supply technology (water quality electronic display board, smartphone app)
  - o Total care service customers can experience in their daily lives
  - o (Water quality check made with visit, diagnosis /cleaning of indoor pipes, safe water insurance)
  - o Infrastructure to improve tap water drinking such as drinking water fountain.

Smart water management can rely on (and combine) a range of technologies. See a comprehensive list in Annex 1. More detailed analyses are required to consider the ones best suited to the Thai context, and the conditions for their deployment.

### 4.3.2. Policies to support the deployment of smart water management

Market mechanisms alone will not provide an appropriate amount of eco-innovation at the right time. This is because innovators may not reap all the benefits of their innovations, and because environmental benefits may not be appropriately valued by markets. This is particularly the case for water-related innovation, where the opportunity costs and environmental costs of using or polluting water are not reflected in prices paid by water users. Since markets fail to deliver the appropriate level of environment-related innovation, policy interventions are required. The question then is: what is the best way to support the development and diffusion of eco-innovation?

The development and deployment of smart water systems has been encouraged by a number of Adherents to the Recommendation of the OECD Council on water, such as Australia, France, Israel, Korea and the Netherlands, several states in the US (Arizona, California) or provinces in Canada (Ontario). They have been deployed in combination with water tariff reforms and implementation of measures to encourage efficiency. In Arizona, water utilities adopted smart water meters to inform customers about their water usage. New smart water companies have emerged in Ontario and Israel. In France, incentives to reduce leakage in water supply and sanitation networks have driven the diffusion of smart meters and investment in data monitoring to detect and locate anomalies in real time (OECD, 2021[5]).

In Israel, water policies illustrate the benefit of economic instruments (fines for water leakage, or tariffs that reflect scarcity) to support the deployment of smart water technologies:

- Water loss fines for municipalities at a level of above 12% water loss created incentives for development of water loss detection and dynamic water pressure equipment. The 12% ratio is particularly stringent, reflecting water scarcity in a semi-arid country (OECD, 2017[9]). It could be adjusted to local contexts in Thailand, in particular to the situation in the EEC.

- Several consecutive years of drought led to a significant increase in water prices. In 2009, an additional "surplus use" fee has been imposed on domestic uses, to discourage excessive water consumption. During these years, one could observe establishment of many water technology start-ups and also implementation of technologies at all scales – from home water-saving devises to accurate reading of water meters to establishment of new desalination plants (OECD, 2017[9]).

It should be noted that, as for any environment-related innovation, environmental performance is best rewarded when the policy framework reflects the environmental externality (the cost for the community of pressures on the environment, such as water scarcity and water pollution). Therefore, as the case of Israel illustrates, water charges that fully cover the costs of supply (including the opportunity costs) are required to make smart water management attractive for users.

In addition to economic regulation and instruments, smart water management benefits from involvement of water users in the definition of services that suit their needs. It also requires appropriate capacity in operators of water and sanitation services.

## 4.4. Blended finance for water supply and sanitation services

Investments in water and sanitation services and water resources management have historically been financed by the public sector, with concessional finance playing an important role in developing countries. The mobilisation of private finance for the water sector has been limited to date. Risk-return considerations and structural issues related to profitability of operating business models often undermine commercial investment. While finance from domestic public budgets and development finance, particularly concessional finance, will continue to have an important role to play in the sector, these flows are not sufficient to address total financing needs (OECD, 2019[10]). It is estimated that Thailand needs 6.9 billion USD investment to reach SDG6 by 2030, including a potential private sector investment opportunity of 0.7 billion USD (World Bank, 2016[11]).

Blended finance could play a critical role in mobilising the commercial finance required as well as strengthening the financing systems upon which water–related investments rely. The OECD defines blended finance as the strategic use of development finance for the mobilisation of additional finance towards sustainable development in developing countries. Blended finance can add value by shifting funds that are currently not directed to sustainable development in countries and sectors that have significant investment needs in order to deliver on the SDGs (OECD, 2019[10]). For example, blended finance instruments can be guarantees, syndicated loans, technical assistance provided in-kind or grants and direct investments in utilities.

As the next section explains, operational efficiency is a condition to attract commercial finance and for making blended finance materialise for WSS.

### 4.4.1. The enabling environment for blended finance for water-related investments

Blended finance cannot compensate for an unfavourable enabling environment, but rather needs to be accompanied by efforts to promote a stable and conducive policy environment. A weak enabling environment characterised by poorly-designed or absent regulation, policies (e.g. water prices and tariffs), or institutional arrangements, compounded by political interference in the management of utilities, constrains commercial investment (OECD, 2019[10]). This section summarizes some commonalities among the key conditions identified which are relevant for Thailand (OECD, 2022, FC).

Policies, legal and regulatory elements:

- Laws establish governing, contractual and enforcement parameters for sustainable operating models.

- Financial contracts are supported by statutory authority and contract law precedents.
- Regulatory regime that defines an explicit goal for a defined environmental resource, such as the U.S. Clean Water Act's "no net loss" of aquatic resources. Goals can be forward-looking or can account for prior environmental harm requiring remediation.
- In the case of ecological restoration, contractual means to procure ecological credits to provide an incentive for investment.
- Unwavering implementation of the regulated and agreed tariff adjustments (as well as the annual indexation) is mandatory sustainable, revenue-based, long-tenor debt financing.

Governance arrangements and political support:

- Qualified entities that are empowered to administer programs at national and sub-national levels.
- Clearly defined roles and responsibilities for water and sanitation service delivery and for water resources management across the institutional landscape.
- Political support at the national and local levels, in particular in developing countries.

Market access and financial support:

- Viable local capital markets with established securities laws and regulations are tested and resilient.
- Secondary market trading is well established. Securities firms are subject to standards of integrity established by law and accreditation.
- Federal and or state government investment quality enables market access at reasonable cost.
- A dedicated funding stream can be secured for investment or security support (i.e., guarantee facilities).

Capacity and resources for quality project development and selection:

- Project development resources can be secured and sustained.
- Project selection criteria is established, publicly vetted and reflected in published project prioritization list.
- There is an emerging critical mass of projects in development that can support aggregating models and private investor support.
- Ensuring responsiveness and capacities of local utilities to the demands of the project preparation phase.
- Secure revenue streams and verifiable performance

For water and sanitation service delivery:

- Creditworthy borrowers.
- Revenue streams are established and supported by high collections.
- Cost management and investments that reduce non-revenue water loss.
- Track record of overcoming operational challenges.

For water resources management and ecological performance:

- Defining the basic principle of a credit founded on science-based criteria and a financial mechanism for long-term monitoring and maintenance.
- A metric of ecological success that reflects scientific understanding of desired physical, biological and chemical outcomes, applied in a predictable, consistent manner for a given resource type.
- Monitoring and information generation to allow for adequate decision making, effective implementation as well as adaptive management and institutional learning. This includes impact

monitoring to demonstrate the long term impact and financial returns, drawing on rigorous data collection in collaboration with constituents and scientific partners

- The principle that private investment in restoration must provide results before sales can occur and a profit obtained.

### 4.4.2. The challenges of blended finance for water-related investments

Blended finance[6] models to mobilise additional commercial finance for water-related investments are emerging but have not reached scale. The analysis of water and sanitation utilities, off-grid sanitation, multipurpose water infrastructure and landscape-based approaches shows that this assessment varies by subsector given the heterogeneity of the operating models in each of them. In general, blended finance should aim to have a transitory nature over the long-run that works towards scaling the total financing available by crowding in commercial finance at a transaction level. By doing so, it enables a capital market building process. Within this process, there are several stages, which characterise the interaction of development/public and commercial finance. Over time, there should be a shift from purely concessional development finance, to blending concessional development finance with non-concessional development finance (e.g. the blending of a donor grant facility with a development finance from public and private actors), to crowd in commercial finance.

For water and sanitation-related investments, the public sector will likely continue to play a significant role in financing due to the public good dimensions of the sector. Shifting towards an increasing share of commercial finance in the sector can not only increase the total amount of financing available, but also strengthen the financing systems on which these investments rely and put the sector on a more sustainable footing.

The success of blended finance is dependent on the ability to mobilise domestic commercial investment tailored to the local context. In general, blended finance should aim to build local capital markets by working with and mobilising local financiers, as highlighted in the OECD DAC Blended Finance Principles. Water and sanitation services are, by definition, locally sourced and provided; water resources are best managed at the basin scale. At the same time, the sector requires strong public regulation due to the public good dimension of water and sanitation services and the common pool nature of water resources. These characteristics emphasise the need to work closely with local actors and align with local development needs.

To effectively tailor blended finance models for water-related investments, an understanding of the underlying business models and value chains is needed. Blended finance models can enter the sector at different points along the value chain, for example at the water provision or treatment level, downstream at the end-user level or at the investor level. Effective blended finance approaches take into account the underlying business models and respective revenue streams, and incorporate different stakeholder perspectives.

Pooling projects could be an effective way forward to address unfavourable project attributes. Providing commercial investors access to a variety of different transactions in the water and sanitation sector can mitigate concerns around small ticket size, risk exposure, limited sector or regional knowledge as well as high transaction costs. Pooling mechanisms - such as blended finance funds - tailor different risk and return profiles for individual investors, with development financiers often taking first loss and junior tranches buffering the risk for commercial investors in the senior tranches. Guarantees, moreover, can strategically mitigate portfolio risk.

Blended finance will not fix issues in underlying business models. Beyond addressing a financing gap, it is a transitory market building tool that is designed to enable stand-alone commercial investment in the long-run. It does so by providing confidence, capacities and track record in markets where commercial investors are not yet present. Blended finance, starting with concessional elements, should phase out over time and ultimately exit in order to prevent market distortion. An analysis of the exit strategy should be integrated in any programme design.

### 4.4.3. Blended finance for water and sanitation utilities

Water and sanitation utilities are relatively heterogeneous depending on the specific context of service provision. Thailand presents significant differences in the characteristics of utilities, particularly between urban and rural areas (East Water vs Provincial Waterworks Authorities). Large-scale, centralised water and sanitation utilities tend to serve large urban areas such as Metropolitan Waterworks Authority, while small-scale, decentralised operators tend to be major service providers to low income households in rural communities such as local government authorities. Low-income households often make up the majority of under-served communities across both urban and rural areas.

Blended finance for water and sanitation utilities can take multiple forms (credit lines, credit enhancements, grants, etc.) depending on contexts (urban and rural; large and smaller operators). Instruments can be introduced upstream, at the level of the lender or utility (technical assistance, loans, credit lines, risk-reducing guarantees), or downstream to customers (utility-based pro-poor financing schemes, access to microfinance loans). It is often accompanied by technical assistance at all stages of the project (OECD, 2019[10]).

**Guarantees** are the most commonly used credit enhancing tool in the blended financing of water and sanitation utilities. Guarantees can lower both the political and commercial risk of lending to utilities. In a guaranteed arrangement, the guarantor agrees to their obligation to service the loan in the event that the borrower cannot repay. This obligation limits incurring losses for the commercial lenders, thereby increasing their willingness to finance a project. The Philippine Water Revolving Fund (PWRF) had primary and secondary guarantees in place: a credit risk guarantee provided participating banks with a partial guarantee from the Local Government Unit Guarantee Corporation (LGUGC) - a private entity - that covered a maximum of 85% of the bank's exposure against a 1% guarantee fee. This primary guarantee was backed (up to 50% of the LGUGC's exposure) by a co-guarantee from the USAID Development Credit Authority.

**Credit enhancement** can be a powerful tool to allow existing revenue streams to be used as collateral.

Another effective pooling mechanism in mobilising commercial finance is through **investment funds or collective investment vehicles**. Funds pool resources to invest in specific sectors (or regions) using different type of instruments, including equity, debt or guarantees. For instance, the USD 234 million Philippine Water Revolving fund blends domestic public funds of the Development Bank of the Philippines which received a concessional loan from Japan International Cooperation Aid, with commercial financing from finance institutions at a 75%-25% ratio from each source respectively. This set up aims at sharing risk-return profiles, lower borrowing costs, and to market water and sanitation projects to private finance institutions. The Philippine Water Revolving fund revolves principal repayments on the loans while interest rates payments service blended contributions from the Development Bank of the Philippines and local banks. In order to mitigate the liquidity risks of the banks involved, the Development Bank of the Philippines uses the loan from Japan International Cooperation Aid to create a credit line that the bank can rely on to disburse its share of the blended loans.

**Credit lines** are a conditional avenue to provide private financial institutions with capital to on-lend to water and sanitation projects. Furthermore, by providing utilities with access to dedicated commercial financing, the long-term aim is to enable them to build the capacity and creditworthiness they need to attract market based financing.

In the majority of cases, **technical assistance**, provided in kind or through grants, is an integral part of blended finance arrangements. Technical assistance can play a key role in boosting investor confidence at multiple levels:

- In the project preparation phase, technical assistance can support government institutions with policy advice.

- Assessing the profitability of a project, by providing support to commercial financiers through capacity building. The concessional nature of the technical assistance grant is critical in addressing the capacity gap of financial institutions in better assessing project proposals, and its cost will need to be shared between the borrower and lenders in the context of phasing out of the blended finance arrangement over time.

- Building capacity, technical assistance is often deployed to enhance utilities' creditworthiness capacity. Such assistance can be effective at reducing water losses, improving billing and collection rates, and improving the management of the utility.

- Generating demand and increasing number of paying customers.

Beyond improvements in the operational and financial management of utilities, technical assistance and grants can support utilities in developing pro-poor pricing schemes. As part of the Facilitated Access to Finance project in Cambodia, development finance providers offered subsidies to reduce the cost of the connection for low-income households. In order to incentivise water service providers and ensure that low-income households had access to a continuous water supply with functioning metering, the water service providers received a pro-poor subsidy on an output-based basis. They had to charge the lower fee to the household, and could only claim the subsidy once the connection had been established, and the metered connection verified. The implementation of financing schemes adapted to the needs of the poor can further enlarge the utility's customer base, in turn increasing its financial sustainability.

### 4.4.4. Blended finance for multipurpose water infrastructure and landscape based approaches

Multipurpose water infrastructure and landscape-based approaches refer to investments that deliver multiple water-related benefits, which can include cross-sectoral benefits such as energy production, agriculture and biodiversity conservation. They can be defined as "all man-made water infrastructure, including dams, dykes, reservoirs and associated irrigation canals and water distribution networks, which are used or may be used for multiple purposes, for economic, social and environmental activities". While they may be designed for a single purpose, in practice, water is used in a multi-faceted way and as such, they can be multi-purpose by either design or practice (OECD, 2019[10])

Landscape-based approaches refer to projects within a given spatial area (e.g. catchment or basin), which often incorporate nature-based solutions. These are emerging approaches which complement traditional approaches to water-related investments that can deliver cross-sectoral benefits. These approaches may include investments to protect and manage watersheds - areas of land that drain rainwater or snow into one location such as a stream, lake or wetland. They include projects that prevent pollution, hydrological risks, such as floods and droughts, erosion and run-off that negatively effects the quality and quantity of water used for drinking water supply, agriculture, industry, ecosystems and habitats (OECD, 2019[10]).

Even within the subsector of multi-purpose water infrastructure and landscape-based approaches, there is great variation in terms of project types, and as a result risk and return characteristics. Given the large size of most multipurpose water infrastructure projects, these are typically financed by setting up special purpose vehicles owned by a consortium of project sponsors that can raise further debt funding if needed. Special purpose vehicles are set up for the sole purpose of financing, building and potentially running the infrastructure project. These companies are of limited recourse to their owners' assets and hence depend on the quality and cash flows of the asset. As such, multipurpose water infrastructure projects are not different to other infrastructure projects and hence appeal to commercial investors that seek long-term opportunities at scale (OECD, 2019[10]).

Commercial investors value projects with a power element, such as hydropower production, in part because of the predictable business case of revenue streams associated with such infrastructure projects. That is, tariffs and power purchase agreements for electricity produced can provide private investors with a clear idea of the project funding. For example, the Nam Theun 2 power station in Lao is funded via a power purchase agreement between the Electricity Generating Authority of Thailand and Electricity de Lao, a state owned utility. In such cases, off-taker or counterparty risk is driven by the public sector's ability to honour contractual obligations (OECD, 2019[10]).

Other business risks refer to market risk (also often referred to as demand risk) associated with a varying demand for the water-related services. In addition, such projects are often not without substantial macroeconomic risks. While not unique to the water sector, foreign currency risks often make the participation of private sector investors in infrastructure projects challenging. Infrastructure projects are often funded in local currencies. However, a large portion of infrastructure projects are still financed in US dollars, resulting in volatile debt servicing cash flow needs (OECD, 2019[10]).

Blended finance models in this subsector apply a whole range of instruments and mechanisms to mobilise commercial finance in this subsector.

Within multipurpose water infrastructure projects, development actors engage in providing equity and debt, underwrite guarantees to mitigate risk for commercial financiers, or provide viability gap grant funding with ambition to mobilise commercial financing typically from local and international financial institutions; sponsor equity is often sourced from private or public utility companies (OECD, 2019[10])..

Multipurpose water infrastructure projects have the potential to mobilise commercial finance from banks and institutional investors as they present a familiar business case for such type of investors. Particularly large scale projects with clear revenue streams such hydropower or largescale wastewater treatment plants can attract financing from institutional investors (OECD, 2019[10]).

Large-scale infrastructure projects should include an assessment of potential negative environmental and social impacts during the project preparation stage, design and implementation. Programmes should be implemented to mitigate these risks and progress consistently monitored. While this requires additional resources it is essential to ensure that potentially negative effects such as displaced persons, ecosystem and wild life damage and potential threats to water quality are identified and addressed (OECD, 2019[10]). Box 4.1 presents the case study for Nam Theun 2 power station in Lao.

Box 4.1. Nam Theun 2 power station in Lao blended finance case study

Strategic direct investments in projects finance vehicles via loans or equity can be an effective tool to mobilise private capital.

This was the case with Nam Theun 2. Total project volume of the SPV Nam Theun 2 is more that USD 1 300 million of which 85% is commercially financed. The complexity is reflected in the total of 27 institutions including MDBs, DFIs, Export Credit Agencies (ECAs) and Thai Banks involved. The SPV Nam Theun 2 Power Company is owned by Lao Holding State Enterprise (LHSE), a state-run business, which helped to mobilise USD 327.5 million of private investments in equity. The LHSE has in turn raised a combination of debt (e.g. AFD, EIB and ADB) and grant funding (AFD, World Bank's IDA). Debt is raised in both LCY by local banks and USD by international lenders, which overall reduces the currency volatility risk for the project company. Also, this large-scale project received grant funding and technical assistance for project development from the World Bank.

The experience of Nam Theun 2 has shown that a co-ordinated approach can help mitigate negative impacts if it is strongly integrated into project planning and financing. Most explicitly, the project is a key part of the government's poverty reduction strategy with an agreement in place between the World Bank and the government that revenues generated from the project would be invested in poverty reduction and public services. However, the additionally of revenues as result of revenues as opposed to previously planned budget increases was not verified. This was in part due to the lack of baseline data and changes in budget classification. Therefore, it is unknown whether revenues replaced planned government expenditure increases. Efforts have been made to increase transparency with revenue statements shared with the World Bank and State Audit Office as well as audits of projects funded by revenues.

The 2017 assessment following the closure of the environmental and social programme concluded that the environmental targets around watershed management, water quality and species protection had been met. The report found that 100% of displaced persons had been resettled and 97% villages met income targets - the rural poverty line which was approximately double pre-project incomes. The remaining 3 % received additional in-kind support. In addition 100 000 people lived downstream and were potentially vulnerable to the project induced changes. A programme to compensate for lost land and provide infrastructure and livelihood training, and a fund to provide investments for livelihoods was created by the World Bank. However, the complexity, large scale, long lifetime and the variety of actors involved undermine a comprehensive and causal assessment of the full negative or positive impacts upon downstream users.

Source: OECD (2019), Making Blended Finance Work for Water and Sanitation: Unlocking Commercial Finance for SDG 6, OECD Studies on Water, OECD Publishing, Paris, https://doi.org/10.1787/5efc8950-en.

### 4.4.5. Requisites to further deploy blended finance for water-related investment in Thailand

Should Thailand further explore the benefits of blended finance for water-related investments, the following recommendations might be helpful.

- Design blended finance in conjunction with efforts to improve the enabling environment

Blended finance cannot compensate for an unfavourable enabling environment, but rather needs to be accompanied by efforts to promote a stable and conducive policy environment. Due to the public good dimension of services provided and the monopolistic characteristics of service provision, the sector requires a strong regulatory and policy framework to function well. Moreover, water resources are a common pool resource, which requires robust allocation arrangements as well as policies and regulations to manage water quantity and quality. A weak enabling environment characterised by poorly designed or absent regulation, policies settings (e.g. water prices and tariffs), or institutional arrangements, compounded by political interference in the management of (often public) utilities, constrains commercial investment (OECD, 2020[12]).

Supportive policy reforms can increase water service providers' credit worthiness required to attract blended finance. For example, the government of the Philippines implemented policy reforms in the water and sanitation sector, including Republic Act 9275 in support of the implementation of the Clean Water Act and Executive Order 279, which shifts financing of creditworthy utilities to market and cost-based lending from banks. These regulations were instrumental in transferring utilities' demand for financing away from public sources. This not only avoided the crowding out effect, but also encouraged commercial financiers to extend their portfolio, diversifying their risk profiles and strengthening their capacity. While the stimulated private sector lending, continuing this innovative financing scheme depends on efficient implementation of policy reforms and market conditions (OECD, 2020[12]).

- Increase transparency to make a valid business case for commercial investment

Commercial investors are cautious about uncertainty regarding any of the risks related to an investment opportunity. With adequate contractual arrangement or blended instruments and mechanisms, it is possible to mitigate a variety of risks, share the remainder with the public sector or commercial co-investors, or take a certain level of risk on the financier's own book. However, in order to make such an assessment, risks associated with an investment should be transparent and quantifiable (OECD, 2020[12]).

- Establish policy-level co-ordination and co-operation processes for blended finance

An excessive reliance on concessional finance can inadvertently crowd out commercial finance, creating market distortions that impede greater accountability and financial sustainability of the sector. Co-ordination and co-operation among development finance actors on their blended finance engagements is a key for the market building aspect of blended finance, particularly when a concessional element is involved. Development financiers should co-ordinate more structurally beyond single transactions. While there is general agreement about the need for improved cooperation, actions on the ground may remain fragmented (OECD, 2020[12]).

# References

Asian Development Bank (2022), *Asian Development Bank*, https://www.adb.org/news/adb-partnership-thailand-focus-private-sector-led-growth-and-knowledge-solutions. [2]

OECD (2021), *Toolkit for Water Policies and Governance: Converging Towards the OECD Council Recommendation on Water*, OECD Publishing, Paris, https://doi.org/10.1787/ed1a7936-en. [5]

OECD (2020), *Addressing the social consequences of tariffs for water supply and sanitation.*, https://www.oecd.org/officialdocuments/publicdisplaydocumentpdf/?cote=ENV/WKP(2020)13&docLanguage=En (accessed on 2022). [12]

OECD (2019), *Making Blended Finance Work for Water and Sanitation: Unlocking Commercial Finance for SDG 6*, OECD Studies on Water, OECD Publishing, Paris, https://doi.org/10.1787/5efc8950-en. [10]

OECD (2017), *Enhancing water use efficiency in Korea*, Environment Policy Committee, https://one.oecd.org/document/ENV/EPOC/WPBWE(2017)9/REV1/en/pdf (accessed on 2022). [9]

OECD (2015), *The Governance of Water Regulators*, OECD Studies on Water, OECD Publishing, Paris, https://doi.org/10.1787/9789264231092-en. [6]

OECD (2011), *Guidelines for performance based contracts between water utilities and municipalities. Lessons learnt from Eastern Europe, Caucasus and Central Asia*, https://www.oecd.org/env/outreach/48656736.pdf (accessed on 2022). [7]

UN Water (2022), *SDG 6 Data*, https://sdg6data.org/country-or-area/Thailand (accessed on 2022). [1]

WHO (2015), *Sanitation, drinking-water and hygiene status of overview_Thailand*, http://www.who.int. [4]

World Bank (2022), *The World Bank data*, https://data.worldbank.org/indicator/FD.AST.PRVT.GD.ZS?locations=TH. [3]

World Bank (2016), *The cost of meeting the 2030 Sustainable Development Goal targets on drinking water, sanitation and hygiene*, https://openknowledge.worldbank.org/bitstream/handle/10986/23681/K8543.pdf?sequence=1. [11]

World Bank (2000), *Increasing supply thru non revenue water, Bangkok, Thailand*, https://iwa-network.org/wp-content/uploads/2018/12/NRW_ThailandCase-2.pdf. [8]

## Notes

[1] For instance, the Background report indicates that non-revenue water (NWR) in the Metropolitan Water Supply Authority (MWA) of Bangkok is approximately 30 % and that of Provincial Water Authorities (PWA) is around 26%.

[2] International experience confirms that private operators seldom contribute to financing. And when they do, they expect repayment through revenues from water tariffs, which are conditioned by operational efficiency and water users' willingness to pay for the service they benefit from.

[3] Issues related to the status of service providers are not covered in the Dialogue as they do not have a direct impact on the performance of service provision.

[4] Here, corporatisation refers to setting up the operator of the service as a stand-alone entity with secured revenues (from water tariffs) and decision making capacity, severed from the political interference of local or national authorities. It does not entail private operation of the service.

[5] This section builds on previous OECD work on the topic. In particular see OECD (2017), which looks into the Korean experience with smart water management in some details and synthesises policy framework in place n a range of OECD countries to promote SWM.

[66] This section builds on recent research by the OECD on blended finance for water management and water services globally. For more information, see (OECD, 2019[10])

# Annex A. Smart technologies for the management of water resources and water services

## Table A.1. An inventory

| Technology, service | Technology overview |
|---|---|
| | i)     Service reservoir |
| Real-time water quality monitoring system | It is a technology built to measure key items (pH, temperature, turbidity, residual chlorine, electrical conductance) using online water quality gauge in the service reservoir and that makes central control system monitor water quality by communicating these measurements<br>* The Enforcement regulation of the Waterworks Act sets forth that "In the clean water reservoir and service reservoir of a water treatment plant of 10,000m³/d or more, an automatic water-quality measuring device that can measure pH, water temperature, and residual chlorine must be installed. |
| Chlorine re-injection facility (Securing pipe-end disinfection performance, residual chlorine equalization technology) | It is a facility that can additionally inject chlorine into a service reservoir or a pipeline in order to address the shortage of residual chlorine at the end of this pipe. It is a system that can adjust the appropriate injection amount, in conjunction with the concentration level of residual chlorine at the service reservoir and pipe end.<br>It is a technology to equalize the residual chlorine concentration level throughout the pipe network by installing and operating an additional chlorine facility in the service reservoir, in conjunction with the control of the residual chlorine concentration level in the water treatment plant, to resolve excess chlorine in the supply process. |
| Stabilization of flow supply (Equal supply) | It is a water-level control technology that can supply water evenly by minimizing fluctuations in production output and demand amount with the intention of securing stable water supply in the service reservoir |
| Integrated energy management (Pumping energy saving technology) | It is a technology that can save energy by optimizing pump operation in response to the changes in demand, based on the prediction of short-term changes in water demand after service reservoir |
| | ii)     Water distribution and supply system |
| Construction of emergency linking pipeline | Pipe hot tapping is built through installing emergency link pipeline (or pipeline redundancy) between service reservoirs or blocks in service area |
| Construction of block system | An effective pipeline network system is built, like managing stable water pressure, monitoring leakage via making separate water flow measurement and distribution of accident hazard etc., by segmenting water distribution and supply system according to criteria such as adequate terrain conditions, water pressure distribution, and size of water supply zone etc. |
| Pipe cleaning | It is a physical pipe interior cleaning (flushing) technology using water, air, pigs, etc. to remove foreign substances accumulated inside the pipe |
| Automatic draining equipment (Remove foreign matter, cut dwell time) | It is a fixed draining system that removes congested water in the pipe as a preventive measure in the congested section at the end of the pipe and the section where foreign matters are frequently generated (It can also be used as a fire hydrant) |
| Anti-rust physical water treatment system | It is a device or a facility that suppresses internal corrosion of metal pipes and removes foreign substances in non-metal pipes through various ways such as using electric, ion, electromagnetic, etc. |

| Technology, service | Technology overview |
|---|---|
| Automatic water pressure control facility (Operate pressure reducing valve) | It is a pressure control valve and a control facility installed for the purpose of resolving water pressure imbalances, such as through water leakage management in water distribution and supply system, and water over/under pressure relief. |
| Pipeline water quality monitoring system | It is a system equipped with a facility that can measure water quality by sampling tap water online for the purpose of monitoring water quality in the pipelines, in addition to a data transmission facility |
| Damage and leakage monitoring system | Pipeline damage prevention system is configured to transmit a signal to its manager in real time when a smart damage prevention sheet is damaged during the excavation caused by other construction work, through installing the sheet over the pipe. Leakage monitoring system is a system that can detect any sign of leakage through leakage sensor that detects the vibration caused by the leakage at night time when the use of water is low. |
| Integrated water distribution networks operation management system (water-NET) | It is an integrated operation system embedded with the function of analyzing data gathered from real-time water distribution networks' water pressure, water flow, water quality, energy (pump performance etc.) monitoring system and abnormality alert; function of making a scenario analysis through hydraulic analysis and water quality forecasting model etc.; and real-time control function etc. Analysis module includes water leakage analysis (minimum daily flow rate, water pressure monitoring, etc.), selection of pressure-reducing valve locations, pumping energy efficiency control, selection of water quality monitoring points, and selection of pipe sections requiring pipe cleaning Real-time control functions include automatic valve shut-off and pump scheduling in case of emergency |
| iii) Water supply facility | |
| Water quality monitoring system for water tank | It is a system equipped with digital water quality meter and data transmission device installed for the purpose of monitoring water quality in an indoor water tank |
| CCTV monitoring system for water tank | It consists of CCTV for protection purpose to monitor artificial contamination behavior around the water tank and CCTV for monitoring water quality in the tank |
| Smart metering system | It is a system based on a smart meter that can measure and monitor water flow rate for individual consumer in a real time or hourly basis. Its purpose is precisely make leakage detection by zone, efficient supply flow management according to consumption pattern analysis, induction of water savings by consumers, and detection of signs of indoor leakage. |
| iv) Better promotion and credibility | |
| Drinking water fountain | It is a drinking water fountain for public purpose that can help promote the safety of tap water and increase the reliability of drinking it |
| Electronic display board that provides water quality information | It is an outdoor electronic display board to provide water quality information throughout the entire process of production and supply of tap water as well as to promote safe water quality. The board is installed at curbside where it is highly visible and offers tap water quality information and other promotional data |
| App that provides water-quality information | A smartphone app, capable of supplying various information regarding tap water production and supply process, is published and distributed |
| Water Coordinator (Quality inspection of water from a faucet) | It is a service where a water-quality inspector visits a consumer to analyze the main quality of water from the faucet and describes and promotes the conditions to the consumer |
| Water Doctor (Diagnostic inspection of indoor pipe) | It is a service where a water pipe inspector visits a consumer to diagnose and assess indoor pipe conditions learned via CCTV and describe them to the consumer |
| Tap water insurance | Insurance to compensate consumers for damages caused by tap water accidents |

## Table A.2. Operational issues

| Purpose of installation | Installation method | Operation method | |
|---|---|---|---|
| **i) Smart water pipeline facility information recognition system** | | | |
| To easily and precisely tell pipeline and facility information without getting the help from GIS drawings | Install sensor(s) over the pipeline or near a manhole | Detect the sensor(s) via a detector (reader) Manage information through deploying a separate operation SW | |
| **ii) Smart metering (remote meter reading)** | | | |
| To learn about tap water consumption by installing it at any region or by block where it is not easy to have manpower to visit to read meters, like the vulnerable class etc. | Replace with digital tap water meter, install the meter, and implement its operation system | Manage information through building a separate operation SW (System implementation is required depending on data transmission method) Gather tap water consumption data and make a billing via the operation system | |
| **iii) Real-time hydraulic pressure meter** | | | |
| To manage hydraulic pressure in real time in a small block using wireless communication technology | Install 4~5 units at main points per each small block | Install once a week for each small block Make an integrated management through improving the existing central control panel | |
| **iv) Small-sized water flow and water pressure monitoring** | | | |
| To monitor water flow and pressure in real time in the managed block (small block) located inside a small block | Install an electronic flowmeter inside the pipeline | Segment into small blocks to examine flow changes and monitor water flow and water leakage Perform an integrated management through upgrading local government's existing central control panel | |
| **v) Water quality meter (water quality monitoring)** | | | |
| To monitor Water quality of major distribution system at a medium block unit level | Install a water quality meters measuring five parameters in the service reservoir and main distribution system | Make a real-time monitoring of water quality at major points in the service area → Prevention made in advance Perform an integrated management through upgrading the existing central control panel | |

| | vi)  Chlorine re-injector | | |
|---|---|---|---|
| To maintain disinfection performance in areas where residual chlorine shortage is expected | Install a chlorine re-injector in the service reservoir (install inside the pipeline, if necessary) | Measure chlorine's concentration level at the inlet and outlet ends to inject an appropriate amount of it at its flow ratio<br>Perform an integrated management through upgrading the existing central control panel | |
| | vii)  Precise filtering equipment | | |
| Crisis response) To respond water quality accidents by installing it in sensitive facilities (schools, hospitals, etc.) in areas where water quality is expected to deteriorate<br>(Water quality monitoring) To measure foreign substances by installing it at major points in the service area | This equipment is installed at the main points of the distribution system | (Crisis response) Check whether it is necessary to replace the filter through measuring pressure differentials<br>(Water quality monitoring) Make a periodic filter check and a component inspection<br>Perform an integrated management through upgrading the existing central control panel | |
| | viii)  Automatic drain | | |
| To block the inflow into the small block in the event of a water quality accident and adjust dwell time to ensure residual chlorine at the end of the pipe | (Small block inlet) Turbidimeter + automatic drain<br>(Pipe end) Residual chlorine meter + automatic drain | Automatically discharge when an abnormality occurs through real-time water quality measurement<br>(Manage proper flow speed in the main pipe by adjusting valve trajectory)<br>Perform an integrated management through upgrading the existing central control panel | |

## Water Distribution Network Operation Management System (Water-Net)

Water distribution network operation management system is constructed for scientific supply management like monitoring real-time flow and water quality of the entire tap water supply process and taking an emergency response etc. by being connected with the proprietary source technology for water distribution network operation management and with ICT. It maximizes the efficiency in maintenance and raises the stability and credibility of the entire distribution process.

## Table A.3. Water-Net

| Item | Details | Actual screenshot |
|---|---|---|
| Monitoring of changes in water quality | Perform real-time monitoring and detection of abnormal changes in water quality by time and system throughout the entire process of supplying tap water | |
| Forecast simulation of residual chlorine | When it turned out that the residual chlorine concentration level is higher or lower than the standard value through real-time water quality monitoring, a review is made on the equalization of residual chlorine concentration level throughout the pipeline based on a simulation analysis, which is conducted by changing the amount of chlorine re-injection such as chlorine injection at water treatment plant or service reservoir | |
| Management of pipe-cleaning section | Through pipe network analysis, the low flow rate section and the water quality complaint point are analyzed to examine the section requiring pipe cleaning and history management is carried out after this pipe cleaning is done | |
| Analysis of water quality complaint | Review is made on countermeasures, such as pipeline replacement, by inquiring and analyzing water-quality complaints by block, by period and by contents | |
| Leakage monitoring | To improve flow rate, monitoring is made on leakage signs of each block, calculate the amount of leakage, check the amount of change in supply and the minimum flow rate at night, and response is taken promptly like leak detection, etc. | |

| Flow rate analysis | Analysis on supply volume and water pressure pattern by block, and flow rate status inquiry and general quantity balance analysis are performed, while managing flow rate improvement project is being made possible by analyzing the daily pattern of the minimum flow rate at night, such as the number of meter replacements, leak points and pipe replacement | |
|---|---|---|
| Crisis management | In the event of a pipeline accident, the module automatically searches for the shut-off valve at the point of the accident, searches for the emergency link pipeline that can be used for the cutoff area, and analyzes the cutoff area before and after the emergency connection is made to quickly respond to the accident and thereby minimize the spread of water damage. | |
| Energy management | Energy analysis is possible to make transport energy reduction, such as analysis on real-time or daily pump performance and wattage, basic unit analysis, pump operation simulation, etc. | |
| Pipe network analysis | Based on the data measured in real time, the behavior of pipe network is identified such as its flow rate and quantity | |
| Schematic diagram | | |

**Real-time water quality monitoring**

- Real-time water quality analysis
- Alarm by water quality standard

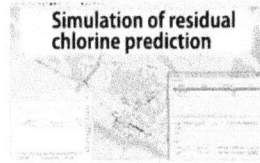

**Simulation of residual chlorine prediction**

- Prediction of residual chlorine reduction section
- Rechlorine simulation (Pipe network analysis)

**Water quality complaint inquiry and analysis**

- Inquiry the number of complaints
- Complaint statistical analysis

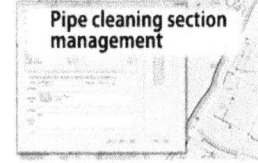

**Pipe cleaning section management**

- Prediction of pipe cleaning required section
- Pipe cleaning record

www.ingramcontent.com/pod-product-compliance
Lightning Source LLC
Chambersburg PA
CBHW081512200326
41518CB00015B/2474